D0595593

I Met a Monk

Rose Elliot

I Met a Monk

*8 weeks to happiness,
freedom and peace*

WATKINS

Sharing Wisdom Since
1893

To my beloved husband, Robert, for everything

This edition first published in the UK and USA 2015 by
Watkins, an imprint of Watkins Media Limited
19 Cecil Court
London WC2N 4HE

enquiries@watkinspublishing.co.uk

Design and typography copyright © Watkins Media Limited 2015

Text copyright © Rose Elliot 2015

Rose Elliot assertedher right under the Copyright, Designs
and Patents Act 1988 to be identified as the author of this work.

All rights reserved.
No part of this book may be reproduced or utilized in any form
or by any means, electronic or mechanical,
without prior permission in writing from the Publishers.

1 3 5 7 9 10 8 6 4 2

Designed by Georgina Hewitt

Printed and bound in Europe

A CIP record for this book is available from the British Library

ISBN: 978-1-78028-836-9

www.watkinspublishing.com

AUTHOR'S NOTE
Names, places, events, and dates have been changed at the author's
discretion to protect the privacy of those mentioned in the book.

Contents

Acknowledgements

This book is the culmination of many influences, experiences and people in my life, and I would like to acknowledge and thank them all.

First and foremost I thank Gautama Buddha for his teaching, to which this book owes its existence, and all those who have practised Buddhism during the last 2,500 years and passed it on to us today.

I'm very grateful to the late Ajahn Chah, who brought Theravada Buddhism to the UK, and whose influence lives on in the monasteries he founded and the teaching given by the monks he trained; and to Ajahn Sumedho, whose books *The Four Noble Truths*, and *Don't Take Your Life Personally* became my close companions, and changed my life. I'd also like to extend my thanks to all the monks at the Chithurst Monastery, especially Ajahn Succito and Ajahn Karuniko. And a special thank you goes to Ajahn Subhaddo for the particular inspiration he brought me and for his patient answering of my questions as I worked on this book.

I am indebted to my grandmother, Grace Cooke, for her vision and courage, and (together with my grandfather, Ivan Cooke) for creating the spiritual environment into which I was born and grew up; my parents, Joan and John Hodgson, for their wisdom, and the very loving upbringing they gave me; also my aunt, Ylana

Hayward, who played an important part in my early life; and to my sister, Jenny Dent, my closest companion in my early years along with my cousins, Colum and Jeremy Hayward, who were more like brothers than cousins and also grew up with us at the retreat centre.

I thank and send much *metta* to my very dear close family, in particular to my three daughters, Kate Ellis, Meg Ashton-Key and Claire Carr, for their incredible, unwavering love and support – and I thank Claire especially for reading the manuscript of this book and giving me the benefit of her perceptive and incisive editorial skills when she was nearing the time to give birth; and to my beloved husband, Robert, my constant companion, who shared so much, and who instigated the days of Buddhist teaching in our home. My thanks, too, go to all the people who joined us for the teaching and made it so special.

In life there are always lows as well as highs when we can learn and grow as we pass through them, and I'd like to express my gratitude to those people who 'saved my life' during some dark and difficult times I experienced in the past, which led me to where I am today: the late Ian Gordon-Brown and Barbara Somers, for their Transpersonal Psychology courses; Beata Bishop for her wisdom and guidance; the late Graham Browne and Babette Hayes for their Self-transformation courses; and the writers Louise Hay, Doreen Virtue and – especially – Wayne Dyer.

I'd like to thank my friends: Elinor Dettiger; Suna Jones, Mary Kennard, Lynda Lawrence, Liz Newnham and especially, Chryssa

Porter, who have believed in this book, read the early drafts, commented helpfully and encouraged me all the way.

I'm also very grateful for the wonderful, professional team I have been blessed to work with: my agent, Barbara Levy, for her absolute belief in this book from the moment I told her my idea, and for her support at every stage; Jo Lal, who likewise 'got it' immediately and guided me in the right direction to make it a reality; the art and design team for the cover, which conveys the spirit of the book so perfectly; my editor, Ingrid Court-Jones for her meticulous work and inspired suggestions; and Deborah Hercun, who managed the project, and all the production team who have contributed to the final result.

Preface

I was just a hardworking cookery writer, creating, testing and writing recipes for my books and articles, getting on with my life with all its usual stresses and strains and ups and downs – and then I met a monk. He came to my home, gave teaching to a group of people – and changed my life. I gained so much from the experience that I wanted to recreate and share it, and that is how this book came about.

It's my hope that as you read this book you, too, may feel you are taking part, and that it may be as life-changing for you as it was for me.

You could read the book straight through or, to make the most of it, you could treat it as a course, reading a chapter each week or at a pace to suit you, following the practice suggestions given just as the participants do in the book.

My wish for you is hidden in the title of this book – hidden like a crossword clue. It made me smile and by the time you've read the book, you'll understand. I hope it will make you smile, too.

So, come on in, and welcome …

Rose Elliot

2015

Introduction

A Monk at My Door

*I*t is early afternoon on a beautiful Sunday in June and a
Buddhist monk is standing at my door. He is of medium
height, muscular, swathed in golden-brown. He has fabric
wound around him over his shoulders and around his waist to
form a robe that reaches halfway down his shins.

His head is shaved and shiny, and he is wearing leather
sandals. Slung over his shoulder like a satchel is a big metal bowl.
I know it is his only possession, used for his two meals of the day:
breakfast and an early lunch that has to be eaten before noon.

I hesitate, resisting the natural urge to shake his hand because
I know that as an ordained monk he is not allowed physical
contact, especially with a woman. So I smile and in a moment
of inspiration put my hands together, prayer-style, and say
'Welcome'.

It is not every day I receive such a visit. The monk has come
to teach a group of people 'mindfulness, meditation and how to
find happiness, freedom and peace'. Well, that's what it says on
the flyer.

It was my husband Robert's idea. Some time ago, when he was
finding life challenging, he began visiting a Buddhist monastery
a few miles from where we live and learned to meditate. He
found it really helpful; in fact, it changed his life: everyone
noticed how much more relaxed and happy he had become.
So Robert had the idea of asking one of the senior monks if he
would give a course of teaching to a group of people in our home.

Robert contacted local Buddhist groups and friends of friends

– anyone interested in learning more about mindfulness and meditation. The word went round and Robert sent out the flyer to anyone he thought might be interested. I did not previously know most of the people about to arrive.

So here we all are. It seems that everyone wants to learn mindfulness meditation. If anyone knows how to do it, surely it's a Buddhist monk – after all, they spend hours meditating every day. As it worked so well for Robert, we are hoping it will help other people, too. I am certainly interested to find out more about it, so I'm open to the idea, although I'm also slightly wary.

Wary? Yes, I have to admit I am. I have a bit of a history where groups are concerned. You see I was brought up in a religious retreat run by my grandmother and my parents, and I also worked there myself for some years before I left. In fact, I wrote my first two major cookery books as a result of the recipes I developed when I was working in the kitchen there. In the end, for many reasons, I moved away – away from the retreat centre, away from anything remotely 'religious' in nature and I became very cautious about being part of any group.

So why am I here today? Why am I helping to host this meditation group? What am I doing with a monk in my home? You might well ask! I am doing it for love of Robert really, because I know it means a great deal to him. And because I am spiritually inclined, even though I am not 'religious' as such. I also believe that meditation can be helpful both physically and mentally, so I'm willing to give it a try.

And that is why at this moment I am standing a few feet from a Buddhist monk, wondering what to say to him, how to behave in his presence, what to do.

Robert, who feels more confident around monks, takes the initiative. As the sun is shining, and there is a little time before the rest of the group is due to arrive, he asks the monk if he would like to take a stroll in the garden before we begin.

We cross the hall and walk out into the warm air. I must admit the monk's simplicity, openness and above all, his ordinariness, touch me. Here is a man who is freely giving up his time to come to our home to teach an unknown group of people, and I am grateful to him.

As we walk in the garden, the monk becomes more animated and looks around him with obvious interest. He chats easily and naturally and I begin to feel more comfortable in his presence.

'Ah yes, *armandii*' he says, noting the vigorous green clematis climbing up the side of the house. 'That needs a lot of cutting back, doesn't it?'

He explains that he was a gardener for many years before becoming a monk, that he has a ninety-year-old father living some distance from the monastery and that he regularly travels to visit him, using his bus pass. I did not realize that Buddhist monks were so down-to-earth and practical.

I look at his bright eyes and tanned face and think he barely looks old enough to have a bus pass. There's a lot to be said for a shaved head. Or maybe it's the monastic way of life that does it.

We go back into the house, through the entrance hall and into the sitting room. 'Oh, what a beautiful room!' the monk exclaims as he enters.

I'm glad he likes it. We spent last evening turning the room into a meditation space, or 'shrine room', as the monk calls it. We moved out some of the heavy furniture and brought in flowers, candles and an incense stick.

We put some dining room chairs in an oval shape around the outside of the room leaving plenty of space for those people who prefer to sit on the floor to place their *zafus* – firm, round meditation cushions like small pouffes that are placed on top of padded squares or mats. You sit on the *zafu* and your legs rest on the padded surround.

At the far end of the room we anchored a piece of burgundy fabric on the mantelpiece with two heavy vases of fragrant white flowers – *philadelphus* – from the garden. The fabric is hanging down in front of the empty fireplace and a large square brass and glass coffee table is pushed up against the fabric to provide a backdrop for a tall, carved, wooden Buddha that we brought back from Sri Lanka – Robert's pride and joy.

I lead the monk to his place at the far end of the room, to the right hand side of the 'shrine', facing the door: the 'head' of the room. He settles himself cross-legged on the meditation mat I have placed for him, with the *zafu* under him. I ask whether he would like a cup of tea or coffee. 'I'd love a cup of tea, please', he replies, 'Nice and strong "builder's tea", but without cow's milk.

Do you have any soya milk?'

I have. I am prepared for this because I have been warned that as a practising monk he is not allowed to have any food after noon and apparently that includes cow's milk. Soya milk, on the other hand, being considered 'medicine', is allowed ... I know, don't ask.

I can't help smiling to myself, though, because I know some non-monastics who would agree about soya milk tasting like medicine. Not me, however. I don't drink any kind of milk in my tea or coffee, but I do use soya milk instead of cow's milk for cooking.

Before the monk has finished speaking, the doorbell rings – the first people are arriving. They're at the door: a tall man called Tim, with short, receding dark hair greying at the temples and a thin, silky scarf knotted loosely round his neck; and a lively woman with short, spiky red hair who tells me her name is Suzi. They're clasping cushions, meditation mats and rugs.

I show them where to put their things, how to get to the loo, where to pick up the name badges I made last night and the way to the meditation room. Meanwhile, a pale, rather nervous-looking young man with glasses arrives, introduces himself as Sam and I tell him where he can leave his bicycle. Then I make the monk his cup of tea.

The doorbell goes again. More people are arriving and this time Robert greets them. I see them coming into the hall as I carry the monk's tea through to him. There is Dan, a rather good-looking, dark-haired young man in jeans, and a woman with long, straight, shiny brown hair, who I come to know as Nikki. She's wearing cream leggings and a loose top falling off one shoulder, looking as though she's going to a 'yummy mummies' yoga class: I hope she's come to the right place.

I meet more people as I come back again into the hall – a tall, lanky guy who proffers a hand and says, 'Maurice'; with his curly, auburn hair and tinted glasses he looks like a member of a rock band. I wonder whether he's got a guitar tucked away in his car.

I recognize a few of the other people who have come: Pam, a tall woman with shiny blonde hair cut in a sharp bob with a long fringe, and an older couple called Rodney and Joan. But most are new to me. More and more are arriving; I'm losing track of them, losing track of the time, losing track of everything. I have a moment of panic: is our room large enough to hold them all?

I try to remember names and match them to faces. There's Ed, muscular, with a ruddy complexion, who looks very sporty; then there's a pale, dark-haired woman called Maggie, who has piercing green eyes and looks as if she is in her mid-thirties; and Gwyn, who appears rather calm and poised, in a silky dusky pink top with immaculate platinum hair and pearl earrings.

Soon there are about fifteen pairs of shoes and sandals at the doorway to our sitting room, and all but one of the people we're expecting are settled within, some sitting on chairs, some on the floor on various *zafus*, cushions, rugs and even a couple perched on low, collapsible, wooden meditation stools – clearly they mean business.

I look at the last remaining name badge: 'Debbie': I don't know her. I wonder whether she's coming. I'm just trying to decide whether to begin without her, as we are already running at least five minutes late, when the bell rings and she's at the door, rather flustered, straggly dark-blonde curls all over the place.

'I'm so sorry I'm late', she says, 'I had to drop my children at my Mum's on the way and then I took the wrong turning off the motorway.'

'That's quite all right', I say, 'we haven't started yet, so don't worry. I'm glad you could come'. I tell her the way to the loo, offer her the name badge, then we go through the door into the shrine room. It seems like a haven of peace in there, with everyone sitting still as if already in meditation. Debbie goes to the last remaining chair and I make my way to my meditation mat, trying not to tread on anyone in the process.

Week 1

Mindfulness: The First Steps to Peace

*A*t last we are all settled. There is a little pause, then Robert introduces the monk and says how happy we are to have him with us.

'Well, it's good to be here with you all', says the monk. 'I hope this will be a time of peace and inner replenishment, an oasis away from the pressures of daily life.'

He stands in front of the coffee table shrine and lights first the chunky white candles and then the incense stick, which he holds between his uplifted hands and raises above him as if invoking a blessing. He then replaces it in the little pot of sand on the coffee table and returns to his meditation mat.

We start the session with a little chanting, using sheets Robert obtained from the monastery. The words are in Pali, the ancient language from India in which Buddhist teaching was written down. It's a bit like Thai, but is no longer spoken. The words express gratitude to the Buddha for his teaching, and to his disciples, who have practised and brought it down to us over the centuries.

The sound is soothing and we all join in as best we can. The chanting seems to bring the group together, although I have to admit that I do not feel very comfortable with it – too much associated with 'religion', for me – and I wonder whether there are others in the group who feel the same. But I have made the decision to go along with things as they are, and I must say, the monk's voice is pleasant and melodious and I let the chanting float over me.

We follow the monk's example and bow our heads at various points, and then we settle down on our cushions or chairs. I wonder how many of the group are actually Buddhists, how many can already meditate and what they want to get out of the group.

The monk pauses for a moment or two, then begins to speak. 'Well then', he says, smiling around, 'perhaps we could introduce ourselves and maybe say why we are here and what our hopes are for this course?'

As usual when such a statement is made, no one moves. The monk waits for a moment, laughs and says, 'Well, I'll get the ball rolling, shall I? And then you can follow if you wish.'

He tells us his name is Venerable Bhante and adds that we can call him Bhante if we wish, though I always think of him as 'the monk'. He has been a Buddhist monk for over thirty years and he was a Zen Buddhist for 15 years before he moved to the Theravada school of Buddhism. He mentions that there is also a branch of Tibetan Buddhism, headed by the Dalai Lama.

He says that Theravada Buddhism is the oldest form, given directly by the Buddha to his disciples in repetitive, almost poetic words. They learned them by hearing and saying them over and over, handing the teaching on from generation to generation until it was written down about 300 years after the Buddha died. The Tibetan and Zen schools of Buddhism developed later, but share the same roots.

'I love the sense of continuity, the knowledge that the words of wisdom the Buddha spoke have been repeated down the ages, helping so many people on the way', he confides. 'And now it has spread all over the world so that Buddhism is the fourth largest religion after Christianity, Islam and Hinduism, and the fastest-growing one in some of the developed Western countries.'

He pauses, then adds with a chuckle, 'That is, if you can call Buddhism a religion...'

There is some surprise in the group at this statement. Rodney, the older man, raises an eyebrow.

'Really?' he says. 'I always put "Buddhist" when I have to state my religion. Surely most people consider it to be a religion?'

'Whether or not it "qualifies" as a religion is a subject of endless debate', replies the monk, 'How long have you got?' He laughs.

'Why is that?' asks Rodney.

'Buddhism does not have many of the things that normally constitute a religion. There is no deity to be worshipped – the Buddha always insisted that he was just a teacher you listen to and follow if his words make sense to you. But you don't worship him.

'He was very clear about this. He wanted people to test his teaching, to try it out for themselves. He told his followers not to believe anything that was told to them, nor "written in holy scripture or handed down by previous generations; only believe in things that seem right and are helpful to you and those around you".'

When I hear those words my tension goes. I feel my body relax.

You really can't fault that approach.

I was brought up in a house where there were such strong religious views – albeit unorthodox ones – that I soon learned to keep quiet and not to question what I was told. This repression continued until I was in my late twenties when all my doubts and uncertainties surfaced and eventually I had to break away from my family to find out for myself what I really did believe.

So to be given permission – indeed, to be advised by a spiritual teacher – only to take his words on board if they feel right to me, is really liberating. I feel happy already and eager for more. I listen intently as the monk continues.

'And over the centuries, although the teaching has evolved, grown a number of branches and spread all over the world, the Buddha's essential teaching – how to find happiness, freedom and peace through mindfulness and meditation – has remained the same and is freely available to everyone. It is something every man, woman and child can try for themselves, if they wish.

'And that – learning mindfulness, and meditation, and experiencing the benefits they can bring – is why we are all here today.'

There is a murmur of affirmation, a feeling of tension relaxing. Then Ed, who looks as though he would be more at home on a rugby pitch than in a shrine room, says that his doctor told him that meditation might help his blood pressure.

'That has certainly been shown to be one of the benefits of regular meditation', replies the monk.

As if a cork has been released from a bottle, the rest of the group start introducing themselves. I try to remember them; names and voices float over me...'Dan'...'tried to meditate and found it difficult'... 'need to be calmer'... 'Nikki'... 'worry a lot'...'might help me relax...' 'find a sense of purpose in life'... 'be happier'... 'just feel there's something missing in my life...'

'Thank you', says the monk. 'I hope you will each find what you are looking for. This afternoon we will look at the very first tool the Buddha gave his followers – what we call 'mindfulness' – and how to use it in our daily life and in meditation. It has become quite fashionable these days.

'Then in the following weeks we'll build on that strong foundation with other simple processes from the Buddha's tool kit and experience the benefits these can bring. But you don't have to take my word for it – you can try everything out for yourselves.'

The monk looks around the group and smiles. 'May I ask, how many of you have done meditation before?' he asks.

Just over half the group put up their hands.

'And how many of you practise regularly: every day or most days?'

Many of the hands go down and there is a little laughter.

'So,' he says, 'most of you are new, or fairly new, to meditation?'

There is a sound of affirmation from the group, then Maggie, the pale woman with dark hair and green eyes at the far end of the room, puts up her hand.

'Yes?' asks the monk, smiling.

'I am a little confused. People often talk about "meditation", "mindfulness" and "mindfulness meditation", and I'm not really sure what they mean or what meditation really is – and how "mindfulness meditation" is different from just, well, plain "meditation"?'

'A good question', replies the monk. 'I will explain. The word "meditation" means many different things to different people. To meditate can simply mean to ponder or reflect, and it can also refer to a wide variety of techniques including relaxation, guided visualization, "mantra" meditation – where you repeat a word or a sound to help you achieve a state of peace, as in transcendental meditation – or in types of meditation where you focus intensely on a particular object, and others. But the type of meditation the Buddha taught, and the one that we are going to learn and practise, has become known as "mindfulness meditation".'

Maggie smiles and says, 'I've tried to meditate before and I know it's really good for me and I should meditate more often, but the trouble is I find it so difficult to make myself get down to it.'

'You're not alone in that', replies the monk. 'Many people feel the same way and I understand this. We don't always feel like doing what is "good for us", do we?'

The group laughs.

'And there can be a sense of duty about meditation, of having to do it, can't there?', continues the monk, 'We say to ourselves things like: "I should meditate, it will make me a better person.

If I were a better person, I'd meditate more, find peace, perhaps have some amazing spiritual experience". It's enough to make anyone feel grumpy, isn't it?'

The group laughs again.

'I'm here today to de-mystify meditation for you. People are inclined to make it more complicated than it is. It is not something that has to be done in a darkened room in hushed silence, with candles lit and incense burning, pleasant though these are', he says, nodding toward the coffee table, 'and it doesn't take years and years of practice. Anyone can do it. So we will take it step by step and by the end of this course you will be meditating like pros.'

The monk chuckles, then takes a slow breath. He looks around the group and states, 'It all starts with mindfulness.'

Mindfulness

'So, what exactly does mindfulness mean? Mindfulness, or being mindful', he says, answering his own question, 'simply means being completely aware of this present moment – really noticing how we are feeling, what we are looking at, seeing, hearing; and accepting it exactly as it is, without judging, comparing, criticizing or wishing that it were different. It's simply focusing on how things are at this present moment – now – without trying to change them in any way. It's being "in the now", as some people say.'

The monk pauses, then says: 'That may not sound like much, but learning to be mindful and practising mindfulness is one of the most helpful and empowering things you can ever do – and *anyone* can do it. In recent years, the medical profession has recognized its value more and more and it is being used in an increasing number of therapies. But you don't need to be unwell to benefit from mindfulness; being mindful can benefit anyone and everyone.'

'So', he says, looking around the group, 'how often are we doing one thing and thinking about another, or wishing that we were somewhere else or feeling worried or afraid of what might happen next?'

He pauses and looks at us all again. I am sure everyone recognizes what he is talking about. I certainly do.

'When we let our thoughts wander we are not being present in the moment, we are not being mindful. We may be hundreds of miles away in thought; we may be years in the past or far into the future, pondering on things that have happened or things that might happen.

'Our thoughts are all over the place, perhaps troubling and unsettling us, perhaps making our bodies feel tense. Perhaps they are even making us miss the joy of the present moment because we are feeling sad about how much we will miss it when it has passed.'

As the monk says that I have a vivid memory of myself in Greece, swimming in a clear blue sea on a perfect day, feeling unhappy because the holiday is nearly over and I am afraid that I may not come back again the following year; so the pleasure of the present moment is tinged with sadness. The last days of my holidays are often like that.

'But with mindfulness', continues the monk, 'it need not be like that. As we learn to be mindful, to focus on what we are actually doing right now in this very moment, we experience the quality of the moment: the gentle breeze on our face, the fragrance of the roses, the song of the birds, the taste of the food in our mouth…we really appreciate them.

'Of course, that kind of focus is not easy to maintain. As we practise mindfulness, we soon notice how often our thoughts have nothing to do with the present moment, how often we get distracted by thoughts of fear, worry, judgment and so on.

'But even just noticing when this happens is a positive step and the more we practise our mindfulness, patiently bringing our minds back to the present moment, the easier and more natural it becomes. And happily, unlike almost any other practice, mindfulness doesn't require any equipment, travelling, payment – anything other than the intention to do it.'

The monk stops, then says, 'One of the very best ways to become mindful is to notice how our body is feeling at this very moment. So let's do that now. Notice the feeling of the cushion or mat, or the chair beneath you; the temperature of your body; any tensions, aches and pains. Just notice them but don't comment on them with your mind.'

There is a pause then Maurice, the guy I think looks as though he'd be more at home in a nightclub, says, 'What do you mean "don't comment"?'

'This is what I mean', replies the monk. 'There you are, focusing on how your body is feeling, and as you do so, you feel an ache at the base of your spine. So you think *Oh bother, my back is playing up again. I do hope it won't get worse this afternoon. I wonder why it's aching again? Maybe I pulled a muscle when I was carrying that case. I really should have been more careful. If it gets any worse I'd better make an appointment with the osteopath – more expense and – oh goodness – I haven't paid off my credit card yet. I don't know where the money goes; wretched government!* and so on.'

The group starts to laugh, but the monk is continuing, 'That's what I mean by "commenting",' and he laughs too.

'We got from the here-and-now experience of the feeling of a pain in the back to self-criticism – *I should have been more careful* – to fears about it getting worse, to worries about money and to complaints about the government. Do you see how our internal comment has turned a simple pain in the back into so much more? And we all do it, all the time – so much of our pain is caused by mental comment.'

'How do we stop doing this, then?' asks Maurice. I wonder what he does for a living, why he is here.

The monk answers,'You focus on how you are right now and, if there's pain, you feel it, but you don't *think* about it. Just let your body feel the pain. Don't resist it, don't comment on it, don't judge it; just allow it to be, just *be* with it.

'Being mindful means bringing our mind back to the present moment, and noticing how our body is feeling brings us right back to the present immediately. Concentrating – really focusing – on what we are doing at this moment, does that too. But don't concentrate so hard that you tense up. It's more an *awareness*, an alertness, an openness, a noticing, an *observing*. 'For example, it's the feeling of the pen between our fingers if we are writing; the food in our mouth, and our chewing, if we are eating; the feeling of the water on our skin if we are taking a shower; the steering wheel in our hands if we are driving. We simply focus on what is real and what is actually happening right *now*, without letting our mind take us off somewhere else.'

The monk pauses for a moment, looks around the group then continues. 'And each one of us has within us the perfect tool to help us with this, to help us with our mindfulness. Do you know what that is?'

He pauses again. There is silence in the group. 'It's our breath', he says. 'Every breath we take gives us the chance to be mindful, to connect with this present moment.

The monk stops, breathes deeply, then says, 'We notice the feeling of the breath going into our nostrils; we feel its cool passage down into our lungs; we feel it going back up again and passing out through our nostrils. We don't try to control it in any way, we just let it be: a beautiful, calming, healing, refreshing breath.

'While we are focusing on that, we are naturally being mindful because the action of breathing is occupying us. In the process we clear our mind; we feel the peace and the strength of this moment; we are fully here, now.

'Let's do it', he says. 'Let's try being mindful of our breath – "watching our breath"– as they say.

The monk waits for a moment. We move a little to prepare.

'Breathe in', says the monk. 'Feel the air going in through your nostrils and down into your lungs; then be aware of it going out again.'

I do it. We spend a minute or two taking a few breaths. I immediately feel more at peace, more grounded, more in touch with my own strength. I am amazed at the effect this simple technique has.

'Why don't I always do this?' I ask myself. My mother always used to tell me to take a few deep breaths before I had to go through any ordeal – but they were not breaths like this. My mind wasn't on them. They were more gulps, all mixed up with fear and apprehension. But taking a deep breath the monk's way feels altogether different. It really does calm me and, in a funny way, put me in touch with myself.

'If your mind wanders, just gently bring it back to your breathing', the monk is saying.

I realize I have stopped focusing on my breathing, and bring my mind back. As I feel the air going in through my nose I immediately feel at peace again, sort of anchored.

'Well, how was that?' asks the monk, after another few breaths, with almost a chuckle in his voice.

'Good, really good', says Gwyn.

'I couldn't feel when it entered my nostrils', comments Ed.

'Just notice it at whatever point you can feel it', replies the monk. 'Mindfulness is about what you are feeling yourself, not what you are being told to feel. Notice how breathing in then breathing out feels for you at this moment. As you practise, you may well find that your awareness of your breath changes.

'So, to repeat', continues the monk, 'mindfulness means being completely focused on the present moment and noticing what is happening to us right now, without getting distracted by thoughts that take us away from that. It's being "aware" without "commenting", or judging in any way. Just "being".

'We can do this by simply noticing how our body is feeling or by concentrating fully on what we are doing at this moment, bringing our mind back to that when other thoughts intrude and, above all, by following our breath.

'How often do we breathe in a day?' the monk asks. 'So how often do we have the opportunity to be mindful in a day? Being mindful of our breath is a remarkable tool. The more you use it, the better it becomes and the more you will come to love and to value it.

'And mindfulness breathing is so easy and so discreet that

once you get used to it you can do it whenever you remember, wherever you are. And you hardly notice you're doing it: you just feel more and more peaceful, happier, better in yourself and more contented with life. Now that's worth a little bit of practice, isn't it?'

The monk pauses and smiles. 'After all, you're breathing all the time; why not make each breath a mindfulness breath as you tune into the present moment, into "now". When you can do that, you'll know true peace.

'You can have some fun with it, too, he says, chuckling. 'You can set up a little "reminder system" for yourself. Let every loud noise you hear be a reminder to take some beautiful, refreshing, calming, mindfulness breaths. For example, there's a dog barking: breathe in, breathe out. Follow your breath, really notice it. There's a doorbell ringing: breathe in, breathe out; someone shouting: breathe in, breathe out; a siren sounding: breathe in, breathe out; a plane overhead: breathe in, breathe out... and so on.

'One thing you can say about modern life', he says, laughing, 'is it does give any number of opportunities for us to practise our mindfulness breathing!'

'You can do it with "worry" thoughts, too. Every time a worry comes into your mind, turn it into a reminder to take several healing mindfulness breaths: in, out; let it be, let it go; in, out, let it be, let it go. The more you do it, the more natural it feels and the benefits to you just keep on building and building.

'Make the intention to be mindful, and you'll find you

remember to do it more and more. The more you do it, the easier it is to remember to do it and the more enjoyable it becomes.'

How to Meditate

'Now', says the monk, 'once you've got the hang of moment-to-moment mindfulness, you can move on to mindfulness meditation.

'Meditation is really joined-up mindfulness, you know. We allow ourselves a period of time when we can sit and concentrate on our breathing. We do it in the same way as we have just been doing, but we do it for longer periods of time.

'By doing that each day, or more than once a day – many times, even, as we do in the monastery, though I do not advise that for beginners – we practise the technique of being mindful in our lives. It therefore becomes easier and we also build up what I like to think of as our "mindfulness pool", a reservoir of peace and strength within us that we can dip into and draw on whenever stresses and challenges come along.

'And, I promise you, it's simple. If you can breathe, you can be mindful; and if you can be mindful, you can meditate. When you do it regularly, the benefits – both physical and mental – just keep on coming.'

'So', asks Rodney, the older man who looks as though he's got a copy of the *Sunday Telegraph* rolled up in his bag, 'what is the *goal* of meditation? Finding peace? Lowering our blood pressure?' He pauses, then adds facetiously, 'Healing the world?'

He sounds crisp and efficient, as though he is going through a checklist and ticking things off.

'All of those, perhaps', replies the monk, laughing, 'but the real goal, Rodney – if there is such a thing as a goal in meditation – is to get to the state where you don't need goals'.

The monk pauses for a moment. We are all silent. Perhaps the others, like me, are trying to take on board the idea of having no goals.

'What I mean', he continues, 'is that one of the effects of meditation is that you become so aware of this moment – through concentrating on your breath going in and out, and experiencing the peace this brings – that you stop focusing on goals.

'There is some research that backs this up. Scientists have found that after you've been meditating for 20 minutes or so you start to function in "right-brain" rather than "left-brain" mode – or to use plain language, you stop being so active and goal-driven, and become more peaceful, more grounded, less full of thoughts, and at the same time, more open to your intuition, your feelings, your creativity, your natural joy – more in touch with the deeper parts of your being.'

'So', persists Rodney, 'how long would you say it takes before you start feeling the benefits of meditation – if you do it every day or most days?'

'There have been quite a number of studies on the effects of mindfulness meditation', replies the monk. 'In one study, discernable physical changes occurred in the brains of those who had been meditating for 20 minutes every day for eight weeks. These people also showed reduced levels of stress generally and better performance in stressful multi-tasking tests compared to the control group who did not meditate. Regular, preferably daily, meditation has also been shown to improve memory, depression and attention span.'

'So', smiles the monk, 'it's worth doing. And when you begin to feel the benefits you will have an extra incentive. People often start meditating because they've *heard* about the benefits, and then continue because they are *experiencing* them, and then they start to *enjoy* meditating ... so it's really win, win, win.'

There is a pause. The monk looks around the group and Nikki, who I've been mentally dubbing Yoga Woman because I have a feeling she practises yoga, catches his eye.

'May I ask a practical question? Is there a time of day when it's best to meditate?'

'Yes', replies the monk, 'any time that suits you and fits in with your life. Of course it's best to find a time when you know you will not be disturbed by other people, so be practical about it and find a time when you can be reasonably sure you won't be interrupted.

'Switch off your phone, and ask those around you to leave you in peace for ten, fifteen or twenty minutes, or however long you need. Then, when you're meditating, if there are noises such as planes, cars, sirens, bursts of music or whatever, just let them be – don't let them irritate you, don't fight against them. In meditation we are opening ourselves to this moment and that means to everything that this moment contains – to "what is".'

There is another pause, then Debbie, who seems to have completely recovered from her late arrival, raises her hand and asks, 'How often should I do it? Should I try to do it every day? And how long should I do it for?'

'Oh my, that's a lot of "shoulds"', retorts the monk, laughing.

The group laughs and Debbie blushes.

'I'm a hairdresser with two young children and a dog, so it's difficult to fit everything in,' she explains. 'But I feel if I could meditate each day I'd be calmer and could manage things better.'

'A regular meditation practice will certainly help,' replies the monk. 'As to when and for how long, it's best to do what is practical and harmonious for you – what fits in easily with your lifestyle – but do make the intention to do it. That is the most important thing.

'Many people find 20 to 25 minutes is about the right length of time and in the research that has been done on the effectiveness of meditation, that is the amount of time that was generally used. However, it's not set in stone; some people prefer to sit for a bit longer, others prefer a shorter period.'

I think of Robert who likes to meditate for at least 40 minutes because he says it takes him quite a time to relax into it, whereas

I can snap into it quickly but find it hard to continue for more than about 15 minutes at the most.

But the monk is continuing, 'If you're new – or fairly new – to meditation, I suggest you start with 10 minutes and see how you get on. If that seems too long to start with, even a five-minute meditation can be very beneficial: there's no pressure, no feeling of "should", about it; just the thought of a few minutes when you can be completely with yourself, tuned in to yourself, noticing the state of your body, your feelings, your surroundings and so on.

'I know it requires discipline at first and feels a bit unnatural. It's like any form of exercise – you need to practise it, stretch that "meditation muscle", and then it gets easier. As you meditate regularly, I think the chances are that you'll come to love it. You'll come to rely on it more and more, to make it your natural refuge.

'My own teacher, the venerable Ajahn Chah – the monk who brought Theravada Buddhism to Europe in the 1970s – described meditation as a "holiday for the heart"'. The monk stops, a blissful look on his face, then adds, 'I love to think of meditation like that.'

After another pause the monk says, 'Think of meditation as a time for *you*; something you can give yourself every day or many times during a day. And remember there's nowhere to go, nothing to do, absolutely no "shoulds" '.

There is silence in the group. The monk's words are giving me a completely new view of meditation. Like Debbie, I must admit I tend to think of it as a bit of a chore – something I *must* do, something that is really good for me but difficult to fit into a busy day. It's easy to find excuses to avoid it.

But the thought of the 'beautiful, healing breath' being always there for me, and of meditation being like a 'holiday for the heart' makes me feel I want to meditate again right now.

'To get back to your meditation', the monk is saying, turning again to Debbie, 'what I suggest you do is forget about sitting for long periods of time for the moment. Just try to fit in a four- or five-minute meditation at some point during the day if you can.'

Debbie looks doubtful.

'If even that doesn't work for you, why don't you adopt the 'short time, many times' approach? That really means being mindful throughout the day, doing little snatches of meditation – say, 30 seconds to one minute or however long you can spare – whenever you get the chance. Really put your attention on doing that, and see how you get on. You may be surprised how your "meditation minutes" add up during the course of the day – and how much benefit you feel just doing this.'

'Do you mean that it's just as good to try and do a meditation minute, as you call it, whenever we think about it throughout the day, rather than sit in meditation for a certain period of time?' asks Debbie.

'Ideally', replies the monk, 'you would do both, but if your life is too full at the moment to allow you to practise meditation for even five minutes, you can still bring meditation into your life with the "short time, many times" approach, or the "meditation minute" as I call it.'

'Isn't that – the short time approach that you've described – just being mindful, really?' asks Rodney.

'Yes, you could say that', replies the monk, 'but then so is meditation itself. It's just a question of the amount of time you're doing it for. I really encourage you to bring mindfulness into your daily life as often as you can; you really will notice the benefits.

'May I ask one more question?' asks Nikki. 'Some people make a special place in their home to meditate, with candles and incense sticks and things. Does that help?'

'You can certainly incorporate those things if you wish,' says the monk. 'Beauty is uplifting and helps to soothe the mind. But I don't want you to attach too much importance to them or come to depend on them.

'One of the joys of mindfulness meditation is that it can be done by anyone, anywhere, anytime. Do you think the one who invented it – the Buddha himself – had candles, incense and flowers? He taught in the forest; he taught by the roadside; he taught in the poorest hovels.'

The monk thinks, then continues, 'You can take your mindfulness with you wherever you go. It is in you; it doesn't cost anything; it does not depend on anyone or anything outside you. I sometimes say to children, "It's like your secret power." How liberating is that!'

'The point is to be free to choose. Our practice does not depend on having certain conditions, but when we do have them we can enjoy and appreciate them. Same with life, really', he adds, reflectively. 'When the conditions are good, we can enjoy them and be happy; but, with this teaching, with mindfulness and the other tools that I am going to show you over the coming weeks, we can still be happy, even when things are difficult. That is the secret of the Buddha's teaching.

'So, in answer to your question, no, you do not need anything special in order to practise meditation. In fact, sometimes we can use the fact that everything is not perfect as an unconscious excuse not to meditate: "Oh bother, I've run out of incense sticks, so I can't practise this morning", and so on.'

The group laughs. Some of us recognize that situation only too well.

The monk smiles, looks around the group and says: 'So let's have a go, shall we? Let's do it now. Make yourselves comfortable.'

People start settling into position: some sitting on chairs, some on mats on the floor with crossed legs like the monk. Some opt for kneeling with their legs either side of their zafu. I try the latter position. It feels comfortable for me, so I decide to stay like this and hope I won't need to wriggle about.

Mindfulness Meditation

'Sit upright on your chair or your meditation mat, spine straight, head level, chin very slightly tucked in.

'Breathe in ... put your awareness on the feeling of the breath coming in through your nostrils ... and breathe out again.

'Keep breathing steadily and noticing the feeling of the air going in and out through your nostrils ...

'Count your breaths if you wish: breathe in on the count of "one"... and breathe out. Breathe in, "two", breathe out ... and so on.

'Or you can count as you breathe in "one-in" and as you breathe out "one-out"; breathe in "two-in", and as you breathe out "two-out"; and so on, up to ten. Then start again or just go on counting, if you prefer.

'However you count, keep your breathing normal by not holding your breath or controlling it in any way.

'You may notice, as you are mindful of it, that your breathing changes, and becomes slower and deeper. There may be a pause at the end of each breath before you take another ... just let it be.

'Keep counting. You can count in cycles of ten if you like and when you get to ten, start again; or you can just keep counting – some people like doing it one way, some another, and it often changes over time.

'Do what feels normal and natural for you ... Keep breathing steadily ...'

The monk ceases talking and we continue meditating. Time passes. I keep trying to focus on my breathing. It's an enjoyable process. Whether it is because I'm doing it with a group of people or because I'm not fighting with my mind all the time but just gently bringing it back to my breath whenever I notice it chattering away, without being irritated with myself – just letting things be – I don't know. The point is I'm liking it and it does not seem long before the monk is sounding the gong to finish.

No one moves for a minute or two. I look around the group. Everyone appears to be serene and peaceful. I wonder how they got on; whether their minds were as active as mine was.

'So, how was that?' asks the monk. 'Has anyone any questions?'

My mind goes blank. Although it was merrily chattering away during the whole of the meditation, now I can think of nothing to ask.

There is a pause, then Suzi, comments, 'I want to meditate, and I understand how helpful it is', she says, 'but my problem is, I just can't concentrate; my mind keeps wittering on and on the whole time.'

I couldn't have put it better myself and there are sympathetic murmurs of agreement from other members of the group.

'Ah', says the monk, with a smile, 'that is the nature of the mind, isn't it? It does that and it always will. You can never completely still the mind.'

There is a feeling of surprise at this revelation from some of the group – and I must say, I am one of them.

'Really?' exclaims Rodney, the older man. 'I thought that was the goal in mindfulness meditation – to make the mind completely still so that you feel peace. Surely the Buddha did that? Or someone like the Dalai Lama can achieve it?

The monk smiles and shakes his head. 'Of course, I can't speak for the Dalai Lama – or the Buddha, for that matter' – he says with a laugh, 'but, no, Rodney. The thoughts are always there and what happens is that you do not let the thoughts distract you. You do not follow them, you learn simply to notice them without getting drawn into them, and so you find your own inner peace that is beyond the thoughts, beyond the chatter of the mind.'

Goodness. That amazes me. To think that the thoughts never go, but you can get into a state where you just don't get caught up in them – and I don't mean because you have dozed off to sleep – is a revelation to me. For the first time ever, I feel as though I really might be able to get somewhere with meditation. I feel encouraged.

Everyone in the group is silent. It seems as though we are all trying to process the revelation that thoughts never disappear.

'So what is the difference, then, between, say, the Dalai Lama's meditation, and, well, mine?' asks Suzi. 'And why am I doing it if the thoughts don't disappear?'

The group laughs a little. The contrast between Suzi with her red hair and tattoo on her upper arm and the tranquil presence of the Dalai Lama is too funny.

'What happens, Suzi', says the monk, 'is that as you become more experienced at meditating you notice your thoughts, but you don't follow them. You feel as though you are the *observer* of your thoughts – watching them, but not getting caught up in them.

'The thoughts that come are like clouds floating by. You watch them pass, and then they disappear and you see the clear sky again. The gaps between the thoughts become longer and the peace and bliss you feel between them, greater and greater.'

The monk pauses. It's as if he's having a bit of a reverie as he speaks. Then he laughs and quickly adds, 'On a good day, that is', and everyone laughs.

There is silence. Then someone who looks a bit nervous – I see from his name badge that he is called Sam – says, 'There is something that is puzzling me a bit. The thing is, how do I know I'm actually *meditating* and not just, well, *sitting* ...?

There is a stirring in the group. His question seems to have resonated with some of the others.

'I sometimes wonder that, too', adds Dan.

The monk thinks for a moment, then says, 'If you have sat down with the intention of meditating and you are endeavouring to be mindful of your body and surroundings and your breath, then you're meditating.'

There is another pause while we all digest this information.

'But nothing much seems to be *happening*', says Sam.

'Let's go through this,' says the monk. 'Are you sitting with your spine straight, in a quiet place away from disturbances?'

'Yes'.

'Then what are you doing next?'

'I close my eyes and do what you said – breathe steadily – notice the air going in and out, or try to ...' he tails off. 'But I get a lot of thoughts,' he continues, 'and at the end I wonder whether I've really done anything at all.'

The monk smiles. 'As I explained just now', he says, 'we all get thoughts coming into our meditation, because thinking goes on. And we all get meditations when our mind is particularly active – I call them "shopping-list" meditations.

'For many of us it's not particularly easy when we first start meditating: simple, yes; easy, no. But it's so worthwhile – and it does get easier, I promise you. You just have to keep at it. Soon you will feel the benefits, both physical and mental.

'You know', he continues, 'there are really two aspects to

meditation: what is going on with your body, and what is going on inside your mind: your outer being and your inner being, if you like, and in meditation we are paying attention to both.

'We put our body in the most comfortable and beneficial position for meditation, with our spine straight, head upright but relaxed, chin slightly tucked in and eyes closed, and we sit quietly for a period of time. If you're doing that, that's the first bit checked off. Your body is resting and, as you breathe, all the cells are being refreshed and they are changing, transforming, in the ways researchers have discovered.

'Then, for the mind, it's as if we are turning our gaze inside us. Although our eyes are closed – most people prefer to meditate like this, and I advise it for beginners – we turn our attention inside ourselves. It is as though we are looking through closed eyes, in a restful way, or as if we are looking through our own forehead. The sensation is similar to the one you feel when you go to sleep, but here you are not nodding off. There's a softness about it, a sense of seeing inward. And in this state we focus as we follow our breath.

'Thoughts come, and thoughts go, but as soon as we notice we're thinking, we put our focus back on our breathing, and so we go on. When we have been doing this for a while, we begin to feel as though we are the *observer* of the thoughts in our head.

'We realize there is more to us than just body and brain; we feel there is a deeper, stronger, wiser, more peaceful part beneath our mind and our thoughts. And then, when that happens, you will be in no doubt that you are meditating. But for the present, have faith in what you are doing and keep going.'

The monk pauses. 'Does that answer your question, Sam?'

'Yes, thanks', he replies.

'My sense is that you are doing fine', the monk adds kindly. 'Trust yourself; "trust your process", as they say.' The monk thinks for a moment, then adds, 'and be a little kinder to yourself.'

Sam looks a little startled, and there is a stirring in the group.

'*Kinder* to myself?' asks Sam.

'Yes', says the monk. 'I'm serious. You know so many of us are so hard on ourselves – we should do this, we shouldn't do that, we've messed this up, we've forgotten that, neglected the other. We say to ourselves, "Oh I'm so stupid, such an idiot. I'm so clumsy. I'm so thoughtless. I'm such a fool. If I'd been cleverer, I wouldn't have done that ..." and so on. The inner dialogue of criticism just goes on and on.'

There is laughter from the group, many of us recognizing only too well what the monk is saying.

'Do you think that kind of self-talk is helpful?' he continues. 'How do you feel when you say that sort of thing to yourself?'

The monk looks around the group.

'Tense', says someone. 'Disappointed with myself', states another. 'That I'll never make a success of anything', offers someone else.

'Exactly', points out the monk. 'Criticizing yourself doesn't inspire you to try harder, does it?'

'But', says Rodney, 'I thought the Buddha's teaching was all about self-control, being self-disciplined in order to improve ourselves. Isn't self-control a good thing? That's the trouble with some of the kids these days, they have no discipline.'

The monk pauses, then says, 'You are correct, Rodney, in saying that self-control is an important part of the Buddha's teaching. We need self-control to achieve anything in life, and that is one of the reasons why the Buddha advocated daily practice of meditation – because it helps us to become disciplined, not just regarding meditation, but in life generally.

'But, what people sometimes forget or don't realize', continues the monk, 'is that along with self-control, one of the most fundamental teachings of the Buddha is what we call *metta* or "loving kindness", and this helps us in our lives, too.

'I would go so far as to say that *metta*, along with mindfulness, is one of the twin pillars of the Buddhist teaching: the two 'm' words – mindfulness and *metta* – they go together.

'Many people have picked up on the Buddha's teaching on mindfulness; it has become a modern buzz word, but they take it out of the context in which it was given, and it is not nearly as powerful that way as it is when you take it as it was intended, along with the Buddha's teaching on metta and the Four Noble Truths, which we will come to later.

Metta: Loving Kindness

'So what is this "*metta*" and how do we "practise" it? Well, as I've already mentioned, *metta* is usually translated as "loving kindness", and it does mean that, but it also means "wishing the best for" or "goodwill toward". So how do we practise *metta?* How do we express "loving kindness" and "goodwill" in our lives?'

No one speaks, so the monk answers his own question. 'It's simple', he says. 'We start being kinder and more loving to *ourselves,* supporting ourselves by thoughts of goodwill toward ourselves and what we are doing. That's what the Buddha taught and it's worked for the last 2,500 years, so I don't see why it should stop working now.'

I am amazed. Here we are talking about the Buddha's ancient teaching and the monk is sounding like a modern self-help book.

'You know', says the monk, 'although this emphasis on kindness goes right back to the Buddha, in recent years they have done research on the effects of it – "kindness research."'

Someone laughs.

'Yes', says the monk, also laughing, 'I'm not making this up. In one study researchers found that the level of serotonin – the naturally-occurring "feel-good" substance in the brain – increased in both the person who *did* a kind deed and also in the person who *received* it. Not only that, but they also found that the level of serotonin also increased in the people who witnessed the kind act. That's what you call a win-win-win situation, I'd say.'

The monk is smiling and so are all the group members. It feels as though just hearing about that research has increased our serotonin levels.

'I really encourage you to take *metta* seriously. It will not only help you to feel happier and more relaxed, but it will aid you with your mindfulness meditation – *metta* and mindfulness, mindfulness and *metta*, they go together, remember?

'One good way to practise sending *metta* to yourself is to be supportive of yourself; compliment yourself, encourage yourself – honestly, why not? This may well feel unnatural at first, but make the intention; do it, and very soon it will become easier, and you will feel the benefits. I promise you that.

'Let your practice of *metta* begin with your self-talk, even if it seems strange at first. Notice your self-talk – how many times you get irritated with yourself and perhaps call yourself "stupid" or any other kind of put-down. Gently notice and then re-train yourself. Many people treat their pets more kindly than they treat themselves, you know', adds the monk, laughing.

I wonder to myself how all this talk about kindness is going down with some of the men in the group. I look across to athletic-looking Ed, who is sitting almost opposite me. I wonder what he is thinking, how he is taking it. He is listening and seems thoughtful; even Rodney seems to be taking it in.

Perhaps the monk hears my thoughts, because he looks up and says: 'So be kind, loving and encouraging to yourself. Remember, "goodwill" is another interpretation of *metta* – the will or wish for good, for happiness, for health. Wish those things for yourself; send yourself some *metta* whenever you feel discouraged, depressed or afraid – whenever you think about it, in fact.

We will learn much more about *metta* and mindfulness as this course continues, and you will experience the power of them for yourselves. But for today, let us close this session with a few minutes of *metta*.

Now you can do this at any time – you can begin or end your daily mindfulness meditation with it – or you can just think, or say, the *metta* words to yourself at any time you feel critical of yourself, fearful, in pain or worried. Try it for yourselves and see what happens. I think you will feel the benefit.'

Simple Metta Meditation

'Sit serenely and softly shut your eyes.

'Take one or two mindfulness breaths. Feel the air flowing in through your nostrils … feel it flowing into you, then out again…

'Allow your body to pause naturally before taking another breath. Follow the natural rhythm of your breathing; allow it to be, without controlling it.

'Now say these words to yourself: May I be well. May I be happy. May I be safe and free from harm.

'Feel the peace and loving kindness healing you, calming you, strengthening you …

'When you are ready, gently bring your awareness back to your body and your surroundings, and slowly open your eyes.'

We breathe steadily; we say the *metta* words; we feel the peace.

The monk looks around the group and smiles. 'Let us close with a little chant to end this session.'

We pick up our chanting sheets and for a minute or two the melodious sounds of the Pali words fill the air once more. Then we quietly move and leave the room.

Quick Review

- Mindfulness means being awake, aware of what is happening in this present moment.
- To be mindful, notice how your body is feeling: focus fully on what you are doing or follow your breath going in and out.
- Every breath you take gives you the chance to be mindful, to connect with this present moment, to feel free, strong and at peace.
- Meditation is 'joined-up mindfulness', a period of time set aside to be still and in the present, to breathe mindfully.

Practice

Practise being mindful in your everyday life by:

- setting an alarm on your phone or watch to go off during the day to remind you.
- choosing a daily activity and doing it with mindfulness, for instance:
  - cleaning your teeth
  - washing up
  - waiting for a bus
  - queuing at a check out
  - eating your lunch
- Do a mindfulness meditation each day: 5 or 10 minutes if you are new to it, 15 to 20 minutes if you are more

experienced. You may find it helpful to set a timer so that you don't have to check your watch. End your meditation with the *metta* words: 'May I be well. May I be happy. May I be safe and free from harm', and feel the peace and comfort they bring.

- Watch your self-talk. Be gentle, kind and supportive of yourself, and don't 'put yourself down'.

Week 2

Suffering? It Happens to Us All

*I*t's a sunny afternoon and we're all back again in the shrine room, also known as our sitting room. The monk is sitting at the head of the room, straight and upright on his meditation mat, his legs crossed in front of him beneath his flowing robes. His hands are resting gently cupped in his lap. I can hardly believe that a week has passed since our last meeting.

I look around the room. Everyone is here; they seem glad to be back, eager to learn more. We are a disparate group. All ages seem to be represented, from Sam, who must be in his late teens or very early twenties to white-haired Rodney and his wife Joan, and Robert, who is in his seventies. To my surprise there are almost equal numbers of men and women, something I have not often encountered before in the meditation, yoga or self-help groups I have previously attended.

Everyone looks peaceful – about half of them on chairs, the rest sitting on *zafus* of one kind or another, while Nikki manages a fine half-lotus position. Clearly I was right, she does do yoga. I wish I could meditate in that position. I can get into a half-lotus pose, but I could not sit like that for more than a few minutes without crippling myself. Maybe I need to practise more.

As I think that, I stop myself immediately. Since last week when the monk suggested we notice how we speak to ourselves inwardly, I have been more aware of my thoughts and have been trying hard to be more accepting of myself, more encouraging, kinder. I must say, since I have been doing this, I have been amazed at how critical I am – I think I've got a long way to go –

hmm, more criticism – but at least I am aware of this. When I change my thoughts and think more kindly of myself, I can sense myself relaxing and feeling happier inside.

I've really enjoyed practising being mindful during the week. I love the feeling of taking a mindfulness breath and find I'm doing it many times during the day. To me it really does feel like the spiritual equivalent of taking a glass of refreshing spring water.

Never one to do things by halves, I have even created a reminder system for myself by setting the alarm on my watch to go off hourly. This means I take a mindfulness breath at least once an hour during the day, although I sometimes get odd looks from other people if they're near enough to hear the bleep.

Yes, I know, it's a bit obsessive – oops, another criticism – but my alarm system is doing the trick and I find, too, that I am beginning to think 'mindfulness breath' at times when I would previously have let myself worry, or I'd get cross, tense or impatient.

I'm pleased to say that the monk's suggestion of meditating for just ten minutes, instead of the 20 minutes that I had been struggling with, has made all the difference to me. I've managed to fit in a meditation every day, even though I've had a particularly busy week double-checking and testing recipes for a book I'm working on, with a very tight deadline looming.

Testing recipes is always hard work; people often don't realize how physically demanding cookery writing is. Sometimes I'm creating and testing recipes for many hours at a time, though the most I find I can comfortably do in a day is five.

Generally, if I can, I pace myself so that Robert and I can eat the food I have tested for our meals, but sometimes it just doesn't work out like that. On one occasion, when I had been working all hours on recipes and had been testing dishes throughout the day, I served the results for our supper and waited for his comments.

He ate, and there was a long silence, so I asked him what he thought of the food. There was another silence and then he said, 'It's all right, but I just don't think it goes together very well'. I had forgotten to warn him that it wasn't meant to. The meal consisted of about six different dishes I had had to test – a "taster" menu, if you like – except I had not planned for them to be eaten all at the same time.

But I'm getting distracted and, as I said, I have been working hard on my meditation and mindfulness and it has been going well. Surprisingly, despite the fact that I have tried various types of meditation over the years with different teachers, no one has ever emphasized to me before the importance of the breath in meditation – or else it passed me by. This has been a revelation to me.

Each morning I have been waking up a little earlier than usual, which fortunately isn't difficult as I'm naturally an early riser. I sit up straight on the floor, wrap myself in a blanket, set my timer for 10 minutes like the monk suggested, and meditate. As I breathe in and sense the air going into my nostrils and down into the centre of my body, it feels as though I'm connecting with my inner strength and a pool of peace within. I find it seems to anchor me inside myself – and at the same time, I feel more open and 'spacious': it's difficult to put into words. In any event, it is helping me to be more peaceful – at least for a few seconds at a time.

I have been counting my breaths and find that helpful, too. I've tried various methods: counting from one upward as I breathe in; counting the number as I breathe out; counting up to ten and then starting again, and so on – who would have thought there were so many ways of counting your breath? But what is working for me at the moment is counting 'one in', as I breathe in, and 'one out', as I breathe out; then 'two in', 'two out', and so on. And while I could stop at 'ten in, ten out', I have kept going.

I have found that the number of breaths I take in a minute varies. Sometimes my breaths are really slow, and I find I take two to three in a minute – this is a beautiful strong feeling, and although I do not consciously hold my breath, I really enjoy the long pause between breaths. I think to myself *I'm conscious, but at this moment I'm not breathing.* I feel as if I have expanded into space, into light; I feel really free and at peace. It is a great sensation.

Other times, I find my breathing is much faster – I take about seven breaths in a minute. I suppose the average is about ten breaths in 3 minutes. When I discovered this, I got quite excited about it and thought I would try and time my mediation by the number of breaths I was taking – 30 breaths for a 10-minute

meditation! One morning I thought I'd see if I could meditate
for 100 breaths, which I thought would be 30 minutes, but I must
have speeded up because at the end I was quite surprised and
disappointed to find I'd only done 15 minutes.

It may sound as though I'm obsessed with counting, but it's
working for me at the moment. I expect it will change. Of course,
my mind is still chattering away, but I have been enjoying the
daily meditations. And the monk's matter-of-fact reassurance
that even the best meditator in the world still has thoughts
coming into their mind as they practise, has encouraged me
greatly. Understanding this, and realizing that the secret is to
view thoughts like clouds floating past rather than trying to stop
them coming and feeling irritated with myself because I can't,
has made a huge difference to me.

So, overall, I am feeling more peaceful, rather excited about
developing this new skill of mindfulness, strangely happy to be
back in the shrine room and looking forward to today's meeting. I
wonder how the others have been getting on.

The monk looks round the group and smiles. 'It's good to see
you all again', he says. 'How did your week go? How are you? Do
you have any questions?'

'There is a question I would like to ask about meditation', says
Nikki.

'Yes, what is that?' asks the monk.

'I was wondering what you think about meditating to music.
Is it a good idea? I have some "meditation music" on my iPod

and I wondered whether it would be helpful to listen to that as I meditate?'

The monk shakes his head. 'That is not something I would advise', he replies.

One or two others in the group, as well as Nikki, look surprised. 'Why is that?' she asks, 'it says "meditation music" on the label.'

'Music distracts the mind', replies the monk, 'and what we are aiming to do in mindfulness meditation is to focus the mind on this present moment, not encourage it to wander off into reveries of its own, which is what tends to happen when we listen to music.

'By all means listen to music, enjoy it and relax to it – but not when you are meditating. When you're meditating, meditate; when you're listening to music, listen to music: that's being mindful.

'Any more questions?' asks the monk, smiling around at the group.

Maggie, who is looking rather pale, puts up her hand. 'It has not been going quite as well for me', she says.

The monk looks at her in a kindly, encouraging way. 'Is there anything in particular that you have been finding difficult?' he asks.

'My father died a year ago', she says, 'and I really thought I was over it. But last week when I was meditating at home, I just felt a terrible sadness. I was hoping to find peace.'

The monk looks thoughtful.

'You will find peace', he replies, 'but you have to "clear the decks" as it were, first. We all do. Meditation spring-cleans us, that's one of the reasons why it is so helpful. So don't resist the emotion: treat it in the same way as any thoughts that come along. Be aware of it, notice it, but let it be. Be the observer of the emotion, as you would your thoughts.

'But I am afraid it will swamp me.'

'No, it won't, I promise you. If you notice it and let it be, you will find the opposite. Allow it to be, to flow as it wants to. Let your tears fall if they need to and the emotion will lessen. And don't forget your breathing: when you feel the emotion, take in a beautiful healing breath. Sense the air going in through your nose and down inside you, as if you were drinking a glass of healing water; and when you breathe it out, let the pain go out with it.

'Try not to get caught up with the pain. Think of it almost as something apart from you – like we are endeavouring to do with our thoughts – and see if you can gently breathe it out.'

'I will try. Thank you', says Maggie. Then she pauses, and adds: 'It also bothers me that I have so many fearful, negative thoughts.'

'As far as mindfulness is concerned', replies the monk, 'a thought is a thought. Let the observer part of you notice it – "ah, yes, a thought" – and let it be. Don't label it as "good" or "bad"; it's just a thought and it will pass. Let it float by like a cloud in the sky. Take another breath and follow your breath with your mind; feel the peace that comes from just noticing it.

'You could also give yourself some *metta,* some loving kindness. Be particularly tender and gentle with yourself. Try breathing in *metta* to yourself as you take the air in, then feeling yourself bathed in *metta* as you breathe out.

The monk pauses, and smiles around the group. 'Just practice, that's all it takes. It is simple, but you have to do it. No one can *do* it for you. No one is going to wave a magic wand over you and make it happen. But you have the power within – we all have – to do it and find freedom and happiness for yourself. That's where the magic comes in.

'And as I've said before, and I'll say again, be kind to yourselves. I'm not joking when I say that this is a fundamental cornerstone of the Buddha's teaching. We all expect so much of ourselves, don't we? And we can be so critical, especially of ourselves.'

After a pause, Ed, clears his throat. 'I have been trying to meditate and I do feel a bit more peaceful, at times, I think...' he says uncertainly. 'But I live in the centre of town and it is difficult to find a really quiet time to meditate. There's always the noise of traffic, sometimes sirens or people talking down below in the street – it makes me realize what a noisy world we live in. Sometimes I find myself getting quite cross and that, of course, defeats the object of the exercise.'

My grandmother used to meditate when I was a little girl growing up, and Ed's remarks remind me of how my sister and I used to have to creep around, hardly daring to breathe in case we disturbed her.

But the monk doesn't commiserate with Ed, he's quite matter-of-fact. 'Modern life, eh? So noisy,' he comments.

'Yes', says Ed, slightly cheekily, I think, 'unless of course you live in a monastery!'

The group laughs a little and the monk joins in.

'Oh, I wouldn't bet on that!' he replies. 'You never know when you are going to get disturbed by something: a lawnmower, someone sneezing, the sound of a vacuum cleaner. And even planes have been known to fly over monasteries, you know!

Chuckling to himself, he continues, 'That reminds me of a nice story about Ajahn Chah, the venerable monk, my teacher. One day when his monks were trying to meditate, a helicopter was circling incessantly overhead, disturbing the peace, and his monks were becoming increasingly restless and agitated. Ajahn Chah, who was completely calm and still as a statue himself, reminded them to stay mindful and said, "Don't bother the helicopter".'

There is silence. The monk explains.

'Think about it', he says. "Don't bother the helicopter." In other words, keep your mind on your breath in this moment now, and just let the helicopter – and anything else that is happening in this moment – be. It's all part of "now" – and in this moment all is well. I often think of this when I am meditating in a noisy place.

'I can't emphasize too often that our meditation is part of this present time, as is everything else that is going on. So, you can never have a "good" or a "bad" meditation (or anything else, for that matter) because your meditation (and everything else in life) is whatever it is at this moment. It is as it is. It just "is".

'So let everything simply *be*, don't fight against anything. Embrace the wholeness of the moment, whatever that brings. That is the way to peace.

'You know', he says, 'one of the ways in which we make life painful and cause suffering for ourselves, is by making judgments and imbuing things, people, events – even our meditations – with meanings they don't actually have, because really, they just *are*. "Oh I had a *bad* meditation!" we say. Or "my meditation today *wasn't as good as* the one I had yesterday." But when we are mindful we let judgment, comparison and criticism go. Our meditation is what it is – and that's all.

'Do you feel the peace that saying, "it is as it is" brings? Say it and there is peace. "I am as I am. You are as you are. He is as he is. The world is as it is." Do you see how accepting things as they are removes the "fight", the aggro, the striving, the pain.'

The monk closes his eyes, takes a breath and says: 'It is as it is and in this moment, all is well.'

'The thing is', he continues, 'the point of the Buddha's teaching is that it enables us to find peace and happiness in everyday life *whatever* is going on around us. We do not have to get away from the traffic noise, from the helicopter, from the world or from anything in it, in order to find peace.

'We have the ability to find peace and happiness within us no matter what is going on outside. We have already begun to experience this with our mindfulness breathing and meditation. And now we can build on that foundation and add some more strings to our bow, more tools to our kit. Are you ready for that?'

The group is quiet. We've had quite a lot to get our heads around. I, personally, have found the mindfulness breathing and meditation so helpful that I cannot think what else the monk could add to improve on it.

But he has a gleam in his eye; he is animated and full of enthusiasm. 'Do you know', he is saying, 'that as an ordained monk one of the things I have to do is to give talks on the Buddha's teaching – as I am doing today – and one of the rules that we monks have to obey is never to prepare our speech in advance or to make any notes. We have to speak spontaneously – that's part of being in the present moment.'

There is some surprise in the group, but the monk continues almost immediately. 'But it's easy', he's says, laughing, 'because the basic Buddhist teaching is so simple and so concise, it could be written on a postcard, so I can always keep it in my head. I therefore don't need any notes and neither will you.'

There is a stirring in the group, a kind of mutual pricking up of ears at this statement. I have to admit I feel curious, surprised and interested. I had always thought that Buddhism was complicated and difficult to understand, so the idea that this teaching is simple intrigues me. What is it that can be written on a postcard, remembered easily and holds the key to peace and bliss?

'It is called The Four Noble Truths', explains the monk:

There is suffering.
There is a cause of suffering.
There is an end to suffering.
There is a path out of suffering.'

The monk stops. Silence reigns in the room.

Goodness, is that it? Actually, although I love elegant simplicity, I'm a bit disappointed. I've heard of the Four Noble Truths before and they have always struck me as being dreary and dismal. I'm really more drawn to positive thought, creative visualization and helpful affirmations that make me feel better, not statements that make me feel depressed.

The monk seems to be hearing my thoughts because he follows up with, 'Some people think that the Four Noble Truths are pessimistic because they mention suffering, but that's not so. In fact, it's the opposite.

'It's true that the Buddha did talk a lot about suffering, but what people forget, or don't realize, is this: the Buddha talked about suffering in the context of learning how we can *free* ourselves from it and be happy! He said, "I teach about suffering and the *way out of suffering*."'

'And do you know what else he said?' The monk pauses again and looks around the group. '"There is no *path* to happiness: happiness *is* the path." Which is what happens when you really get to grips with mindfulness. In this moment now, all is well, all is happy, I am free … ' he says, quietly, thoughtfully.

'So the Buddha's teaching is fundamentally about happiness, freedom and peace, as I hope you will discover for yourselves. This simple – but undoubtedly profound – teaching truly leads to happiness.'

The monk thinks for a moment, then chuckles and adds 'I sometimes think that if the Buddha were alive today and had a PR team they would make him repackage his message and use the word "happiness" instead of "suffering". Something like: "There is happiness. There is the cause of happiness. There is the realization of happiness. There is the way of life that leads to happiness."'

We all laugh and the monk continues, 'Go on, say them to yourself: "There is happiness. There is the cause of happiness. There is the realization of happiness. There is the way of life that leads to happiness.'

He stops again, then says 'You know, when you express the Four Noble Truths like that, they don't sound quite so powerful. Do you agree? They don't really hit the spot, do they?

'It's like when you're feeling really unhappy and someone says to you, "there, there. Calm down, it's all right", and you know that it's *not* all right, you're really hurting inside and what you need is to be able to talk about that pain. You need to look at it squarely, to acknowledge it and have others acknowledge it too, rather than tell you it's nothing to worry about and gloss it over.

'The Buddha never glossed over anything or pretended the suffering didn't exist. He looked at life and he saw suffering, and he found a way to address that suffering – to find the cause of it and to find freedom from it. He called a spade a spade, that's the truth of the matter. He was a very down-to-earth, practical man, was the Buddha', he adds, sounding as though he's talking about an old friend.

'But you don't have to take my word for it; you don't have to take anyone's word for it. We can all try it out for ourselves, just as the Buddha urged his followers to do. We study the Four Noble Truths; we consider them and, as with our mindfulness breathing, we apply them to ordinary, everyday things and situations. We learn about the Four Noble Truths by experiencing them working in our lives.

'The Four Noble Truths and mindfulness work together – they are so closely linked. The teaching is very practical and simple, but it's also contemplative – that's where the mindfulness comes in. To make the most of it, all you need is a mind that is open and receptive, and a willingness to ponder and consider.'

The monk chuckles, then adds, 'You know, I often think mindfulness kind of resembles a protective vehicle you can get into – the car you sit in, complete with shock absorbers – and the Four Noble Truths are like the wheels on the car that carry you smoothly over the bumps in the road to your destination.'

'And what *is* our destination?' asks Dan jokily from the far side of the group.

'Why, *nirvana*, of course!' replies the monk with another laugh. 'So get in your car. We'll take a look at those wheels now, make sure they're up and running and you'll be there before you know it. You don't have to die to reach *nirvana*, you know.'

The monk smiles broadly and the group smiles and laughs. I don't think any of us has ever before heard the Four Noble Truths and mindfulness meditation described as a vehicle in which to travel our path through life, but I rather like the idea and feel ready to find out more.

'And today', continues the monk, who really seems to be on a roll now, 'we are going to study the first Noble Truth: "there is suffering". So let's not wait a moment longer.'

The First Noble Truth

'The First Noble Truth, like each of the others, has three parts to it. The Buddha called these "insights". First there is a simple statement of fact, followed by what has to be done and finally, the result.

'You could say that each of the four wheels of your car has three spokes', he says with a smile, 'if that's not pushing the car metaphor too far.

'In this First Noble Truth, the "first insight" – the statement of fact – is "there is suffering". The "second insight" – the action to be taken – is "suffering should be understood". And the "third insight" – the result – is "suffering has been understood".'

My head is in a whirl. It seems to me that the insights are just telling us to think about these truths until we reach the point when we realize we've understood them. That doesn't seem to be much – after all, we all know what suffering is.

'A Noble Truth', continues the monk, 'means a truth to be reflected upon, not an absolute truth, like some law written in stone. We have to contemplate the Noble Truths and we do this through experiencing them working.

'We apply the Noble Truths to ordinary, everyday things in our lives, to ordinary situations. We experiment with them, find out for ourselves whether they work or not and if they're helpful to us. It's very experiential.

'Remember, the Buddha came upon the Four Noble Truths through his study of life while looking for an answer to all the suffering he saw, and we in turn learn about the Noble Truths through seeing them working in our own lives, as we discover how to use them to let go of our own suffering and find happiness, freedom and peace.'

We are all rather silent, then the monk says, 'I expect you all know the story of the Buddha's life and how he came upon the Four Noble Truths?'

No one says anything, so he continues, "He was born a prince and his name was Gautama. The monk pauses for a moment and looks at Nikki who has a puzzled expression on her face. 'I thought he was called Siddhartha,' she says a little indignantly. 'I read a book about him once, and it was called *Siddhartha*.'

'Yes', replies the monk, 'he is known by both names – Siddhartha and Gautama – and you may also see him referred to as "Shakyamuni", which is based on his family or surname – Shakya. Shakyamuni actually means "sage of the Shakya clan". But let's stick to "Gautama" as it's simpler.

'At the time of Gautama's birth a wise man predicted to his father that his son would either become a great king or a renowned spiritual teacher. The king was appalled at the thought of his son becoming a spiritual teacher and so he did his utmost to prevent him from ever seeing or experiencing suffering, or anything else that might affect his mind in a way that might make the prophecy come true.

'The king gave his son a life of absolute luxury and kept him within the vast palace grounds. But in due course Gautama escaped to the nearby town, witnessed old age, sickness and death, and was deeply shocked and appalled – so much so, that he made it his mission to discover an answer to it.

'He left home, gave up all his possessions and lived off the alms that he was given. He fasted often, but when he nearly died of weakness and starvation he realized that it was unwise to go to such an extreme or he would not be able to carry out his work – he had discovered "the middle way" of moderation.

'Eventually, at the time of the full moon in May, Gautama sat down under a fig tree – later renamed a Bodhi or "spiritual-awakening" tree in his honour – and resolved not to move until he had found the answer to suffering.

'He went into a deep trance that lasted the whole night through. Then, as the moon set in the west and the sun rose in the east, he opened his eyes. He had received the answer: it was the Four Noble Truths.'

The monk stops. His talk of the young Buddha and his life has brought a rather beautiful atmosphere into the room, an almost tangible presence.

He continues quietly, 'The way we lead our lives now has changed beyond all recognition from Buddha's time, but human nature has not. That's why this teaching works as well today as it did all those centuries ago.

'We still have the same suffering that shocked the young Prince Gautama: old age, sickness, sorrow and death. As his teaching – the Four Noble Truths – was based on coping with this, it is as relevant today as it was then. That's why it works so well, and why I am passing it on to you now, just as it has been passed down from person to person through the ages for the last twenty-five centuries.'

'So' he gently asks, 'shall we begin?'

There is suffering

'The First Noble Truth states, "There is suffering" – *dukka*, as the Buddha calls it. No one can argue with that. We see it around us all the time. Everybody suffers in some way or another. The world is full of suffering.

'But do you notice the way this insight is phrased? That is crucial. It is not "*I am* suffering", "*you are* suffering", "*the animals are* suffering" or "*people* are suffering", but "there is suffering". A simple statement of fact: "*There is* suffering." Do you notice the difference between saying, "*I am* suffering" and "*there is* suffering"?'

The monk pauses and looks around the room. We are all sitting in silence, listening intently.

'Try saying them slowly to yourself: "I am suffering" or "there is suffering". Do you notice the difference?' he repeats.

I do notice the difference. When you say "there is suffering", you are acknowledging the suffering – you're certainly not suppressing it or denying it – but it feels as though you are putting a little distance, a breathing space, between yourself and the suffering. With 'there is suffering', it feels as though you're putting yourself in the position of the observer, looking at the suffering, rather than being the sufferer experiencing the suffering. When I say "there is suffering", I feel as though I'm more in control. I like this feeling.

'"There is suffering"', continues the monk, 'is a clear statement that at this moment there is some feeling of unhappiness. It does not have to be extreme torture, though it could be. It can range from absolute anguish to mild boredom. It can be fear, anger, jealousy, envy, nervousness or any other negative emotion you are feeling, as well as physical pain. Suffering applies to them all.

'We are not judging the degree of suffering or anything about it. All we are doing is acknowledging the presence of the suffering. We can name it for what it is: "there is worry" or "there is pain" or "there is sadness", but we do not have to. Simply acknowledging that "there is suffering" is enough. We are not trying to identify with it or judge it or suppress it or fix it. We are simply noticing it, accepting it is there. For example, imagine you're rushing to catch a train. The traffic is slow, then you have trouble finding a parking place. You rush into the station and see your train pulling out. How do you feel? Notice these feelings: "at this moment there is suffering" or "there is impatience/anger/fear/irritation", whatever you are feeling.

'Notice these feelings, but leave it there. Don't start getting caught up in them, judging yourself or the situation by thinking things like: *I should have left home earlier; I'm such an impatient person; I must relax more; it's not good for my blood pressure; I'm afraid I'm going to be late and miss my meeting; they really should do something about the traffic; wretched government; and so on."*

'It's easy and natural to get caught up in a chain of thoughts that just confuses the issue and does not help you to find peace. So keep bringing your thoughts back to the essential core of the situation: *there is suffering.*

'Just as with meditation, you could take some "mindfulness" breaths. Feel the air going in through your nostrils and out again. Feel how that calms and settles you, connecting you with the present moment, with your inner strength.

'Try it for yourselves and see what happens. Breathe in, feel the suffering; breathe out, let it go. My guess is you will find that you are feeling calmer. You will be seeing things more clearly rather than getting caught up in them and taking them personally.

'You will have realized the first part of the First Noble Truth: "there is suffering"'. The monk smiles and chuckles for a moment, then becomes serious again and continues.

Suffering should be understood

'So, having looked at the first part of the First Noble Truth, "there is suffering", and having learned the value of referring to pain, suffering and discomfort in a non-personal way – "there is suffering", rather than "I am suffering" – we come to the second part or insight: *"suffering should be understood"*. The state of suffering is to be investigated.'

Gosh, we could be here for hours at this rate, I think, and begin to feel rather hungry. My tummy rumbles at the thought of food. I wonder whether anyone else has heard it. I feel embarrassed; then I catch myself in time and think: *there is worry; there is discomfort; there are tummy rumbles; there is fear of what people might think; there is suffering.*

I smile as I think this to myself; I feel my body relaxing. I'm doing it. I'm actually being mindful. I'm liking this. I suddenly remember the feeling of excitement I got when I learned to ride a bike: confident, exhilarated, in control. It feels like that.

But back to the monk who is saying, 'When we say "suffering should be understood", we need to remember that in the original Pali, the ancient language of the Buddha, the word "understand" has a deeper meaning than simply "comprehend". It literally means "stand under"; totally accept; bear; embrace: truly "*stand under*" the suffering.

'It is very easy to blame something or someone for the pain and suffering we feel. How often do you hear people say, "You're making me feel bad/jealous/unhappy/guilty?" How often do you hear them blame their unhappiness on their upbringing or their parents? Of course, these things can have a powerful effect. But as we start to understand, to accept that "there is suffering"– to "stand under it", to bear it – we begin to realize that our suffering does *not depend on* what is happening outside us or *to us.*

'Suppose someone is being unpleasant to you or slighting you: *they* are not *making* you suffer. Whether you allow yourself to be hurt or offended is entirely your choice. 'So, become the observer; notice that "there is suffering" or hurt or whatever name you like to give it, then stop there. Stand under it, accept it, bear it. Don't get into a tangled thought web of blame, reasons, justification, anger, desire for revenge and so on. These just stir up and increase the pain.

'Ironic though it may seem, if you want to find inner peace and freedom from suffering, you need to stay with the feeling of suffering – "stand under" it, embrace it. Then, it will go of its own accord, as you will see.

'My teacher, Ajahn Sumedho, even says "welcome"' to the suffering and some practised Buddhist monks send thoughts of *metta* – loving kindness – to the suffering. That all might seem to be going a bit far at this stage, but when you start allowing the pain to be, accepting it, saying "welcome" to it even, sending it loving kindness is just the next step towards inner peace. This is very liberating because it takes away all resistance to what is happening.'

I find the thought of this empowering. I can see that as you take the position of 'observer' of your own suffering – or rather *'the* suffering' – and as you keep bringing your mind back to that rather than blaming a situation or a person for 'making' you suffer, you're in charge of your own state of mind, you're liberated and strong.

The monk pauses, then adds, 'No longer will you need to depend on other people, circumstances, material possessions – anything – to "make" you happy. You will know how to free yourself from suffering and find happiness for yourself. What a glorious thing that is!

'The Buddha's approach is unique because he shows that the way out of suffering is in our own hands – or minds. This is very "grown-up" teaching. Our happiness does not depend on anything outside ourselves. It's all in here', he says, putting his hand to his head and then to his heart. 'We have our own key to the door. We just need to learn how to use it.'

Suffering has been understood

'To recap ... if someone is being unkind to you or says something hurtful, and you think they are *making* you suffer, you have not understood the First Noble Truth. Even if they are torturing you and you blame your pain on them, you have not understood the First Noble Truth. As long as you think the source of your pain and suffering comes from outside you, from "out there", rather than "in here"', the monk says, pointing to his head, 'you have not understood the First Noble Truth. You have given your power away.

'That may sound tough but the way out of suffering is not through blaming, hating or being angry and revengeful with anything or anyone outside you – or, indeed, with you yourself. Those thoughts only hurt you and block your happiness, freedom and peace. The way out of suffering, the way to happiness, freedom and peace in life, is through noticing "there is suffering" then "standing under", accepting and allowing it to be "exactly as it is".

'Try it for yourselves and see. When you do that, as you'll find out, the suffering inside you won't stay "as it is". It will change. Inner peace will come; inner strength and poise will come. You will get to the point where you simply don't notice slights and little hurts.

'Of course, big things will affect you; and of course you will feel them. But as you embrace the suffering without blame, anger or rejection, you *will* find peace – and inner strength, too.

'But don't wait for big things to happen. Start practising now with little things, such as when someone jostles you while you're waiting in a queue; when another driver cuts you up in the traffic; when someone says something hurtful or insulting; when you feel impatient because the kids have left their clothes on the floor yet again; when your partner is so irritating you feel you could scream... and so on.

'There are countless times in life when we can be upset, offended, irritated or annoyed. Notice the feeling, but remember you don't need to be upset, offended, irritated or annoyed. You certainly don't need to "get back" at the person. "Getting back" does not help at all; it just perpetuates the negativity, passes it on like a Chinese whisper.

'Being aware of your own feelings and taking responsibility for them does help. It stops the chain of negativity right there. It frees you, it frees the other person and it frees the world from having more negativity added to it.

'We all say we want peace in the world and sometimes we feel helpless to do anything about it. But we *can* do something about it. Just by putting into practice the First Noble Truth we can create a more peaceful world: peace begins with us, each one of us. Think about it; do it.

'And', adds the monk with a smile, 'isn't it empowering when you realize that whatever others say, whatever they do, they can't get at you?'

Is that so?

The monk is silent for a moment, thinking; then he says, 'That reminds me of a famous Zen Buddhist story about a monk. Some of you may have heard it before, but I think it's worth repeating.

'A beautiful girl in a village in Japan is pregnant. Her parents are furious and ask her who the father is. She does not want to get her lover into trouble, so she accuses Hakuin, an old man and a most revered and respected monk, of seducing her.

'When the girl has given birth, the parents take the baby boy to Hakuin and demand that he takes care of him since he is the father. "Is that so?" is all that Hakuin says. But he takes care of the baby for several months. Then the embarrassed girl confesses to her parents that the father was actually a young man in the village.

'The parents go back to Hakuin, inform him that he is not the father after all, apologize profusely and ask for the baby to be returned. "Is that so?" replies Hakuin, handing the baby back to them.'

The monk pauses for a moment, reflecting, then he adds, 'When you know and put into practice the First Noble Truth, you free yourself from the need to react by taking offence. It can be done.

'There is a famous true story about how the Buddha reacted on one occasion when he was giving a speech and a noisy young man started interrupting and shouting insults at him. "You have no right to teach others how to behave", the man screamed, "you are just a fake master who is fooling everyone."

'The Buddha continued to talk, ignoring the young man who got even more angry, standing right in front of the Buddha, shouting insults in his face. The Buddha's followers tried to move the young man away, but the Buddha stopped them. He turned to the heckler, smiled at him and said, "If you buy a present for someone and they do not accept that present, who does it belong to?"

The young man quietened down and thought for a moment. "I suppose it would still belong to me, because I had bought it", he said.

'The Buddha smiled and replied, "Yes, that is so. And it is the same with your anger. I do not feel insulted by it because I do not accept it. I am handing it back to you. You are the unhappy one; you are simply hurting yourself."

'The young man understood this and felt embarrassed by his behaviour. In fact, the Buddha's reaction made such an impact on him that he became one of his followers.

'You never have to accept insults or anger from other people', says the monk. 'Simply don't receive them; don't allow them to get at you, then they remain with the person who is trying to give them to you.

'How different the world would be if everyone followed this practice! Libel lawyers would go out of business and many wars simply would not get started. Inner peace would truly become world peace.

'So try it for yourselves. Work with the little dissatisfactions, annoyances and hurts of ordinary life. Notice how you can be irritated, upset or angered by your children, your partner, the weather, your neighbours, the government, the cat, the television, the car that won't start – or just by yourself. Notice it, accept it and *let it be*. Don't provoke other people – and if they provoke you, remember who the insult or anger belongs to as long as you don't react to it.'

Accepting and 'letting go' in the work place

Tim, the tall dark guy with the loose silky cravat around his neck, raises his hand to speak.

'You have a question?' asks the monk.

'Yes', replies Tim. 'That's an inspiring and thought-provoking story, but when it comes to actions that have to be taken, I don't see how "letting everything be" works in everyday life. I'm a doctor and if I just "let everything be", the NHS would grind to a halt as far as my patients are concerned.'

'I thought that was what was happening in the NHS anyway', quips Suzi. Tim pulls a face and everyone laughs.

'Of course you have to do your work to the best of your ability, Tim', replies the monk, 'but for the moment I would just say that when I say "accepting" and "letting be", I'm talking first and foremost about what is happening *inside* you. I'm talking about your attitude – the fears, the tensions, the desires that arise in you. The way to peace is to recognize them, to feel them without trying to change them. In other words let them be, and they will dissolve.

'That doesn't mean you can't do anything practical as well, but it means always looking inside yourself rather than blaming how you are feeling and what is happening on anything outside you. When you are calm within, mindful of all that is going on in the present moment and allowing it to be as it is, you are in the best possible state of mind to make wise decisions. And when you're calm and focused, you tend to attract calm conditions to you. Inner peace brings outer peace.

'You don't have to look any further than the Dalai Lama, Mother Theresa, Nelson Mandela or the Buddhist leader of the opposition in Burma, Aung San Suu Kyi, who was imprisoned, to see how they have affected the lives of many people all over the world simply by the inspiration they have given by just being themselves.'

'Well, I certainly don't think of myself as a Mother Theresa!' exclaims Tim with a laugh. 'But I do understand what you are saying. You're talking about what's happening inside us, not about taking a *laissez-faire* approach to our work and responsibilities.'

'That is so', says the monk. 'I'm also talking about not worrying about the world and the actions of other people and not trying to set the world to rights by your judgments, comparisons, criticisms and so on.

'As I have already said, something you *can* do that you will find very helpful for the development of inner peace is to give up judgment and criticism. By that I really mean opinions and views

… perhaps that is a better way of putting it.

'The world is so full of opinions about this, judgments about that, views about the other. "I think this" and "I think that"; "they shouldn't be doing this" or "they – or you – ought to be doing that" and "I like this better than the other." Let all of that go: think of Hakuin and "is that so?" At first it's quite difficult because we're so used to having opinions and views, and making judgments. But once you start watching yourself, you will realize how much you do it and you will be amazed how much more peaceful you feel when you stop.

'Like all of the things I'm putting before you, it takes a bit of practice. But the more you do it – the more you let go of judgments, opinions and criticism, and particularly taking offence – the more natural it feels. And the greater your own sense of happiness, freedom and peace and the greater the happiness, freedom and peace around you.'

The monk looks at the group members, then says, 'Giving up opinions, criticism, comparisons and judgments is a small price to pay for the peace you will feel, you know – and the peace you will bring to the world. I really encourage you to do this simple thing. Just start; it will soon become a habit and once you experience the peace this brings, you'll never want to go back.

'Inner peace, world peace,' says Pam.

'Yes, indeed', replies the monk, 'yes indeed'.

The monk looks around the group members.

'Is that everything?' he asks.

'Then, let's close this session with a little meditation. This time we will start by being mindful of both our breath and our body.

Meditation

'Make yourselves comfortable. Sit upright but don't worry about your position; be natural.

'Relax your hands and rest them gently cupped in your lap or on your thighs.

'Your eyes can be closed, or open or half open, looking a few feet ahead not focusing on anything ... do whatever is comfortable for you.

'Concentrate on your breathing: your breath going in through your nose, flowing into your lungs, then out through your nose ...

'Be aware of the ground beneath you, supporting you.

'Be mindful of your body; if you can feel any any tension, just let it go ... in your head ... your eyes... jaw ... neck ... shoulders ... your chest ... arms ... hands ... fingers ... your abdomen ... hips ... thighs ... legs ... your feet and toes ...

'Let go of your worries and cares ... let go of the thoughts and the emotions attaching to them; just let them go and allow the feeling or the desire, to be ...

'When your mind wanders, bring it back to here and now, to the feeling of the ground beneath you, to your breathing ...

'Bring your attention back to the present ... notice the feeling you have of stress, of wanting or not wanting, of trying to make things different from the way they are ... notice it and allow everything to be the way it is ...

'When you do that, when you let go of your desires and the emotions attaching to them, when you let it all be exactly as it is, what happens?

'Well, try it for yourself and see ...'

We continue for about 20 minutes, then the monk sounds the gong.

We gently bring our awareness back to our surroundings and open our eyes, but no one moves. We are still for a while. It is as if we all want to experience the beautiful feeling for a little longer.

The monk puts his hands into prayer position and touches them to his head and then to his heart. We move, we stretch our legs and then we quietly pick up our things. The session is ended and we all leave the room.

Quick review

- Life is full of pain – "there is suffering" – but you do not have to suffer.
- When you feel a painful thought, take a mindfulness breath and simply observe the thought; don't judge or elaborate on it.
- Say to yourself: 'there is suffering' – not 'I am suffering'.
- Continue with this practice every time the thought comes into your mind and feel the suffering gradually lessen its grip on you.
- You will no longer blame suffering on anything outside yourself, you will be *free*.

Practice

- Practise the First Noble Truth, remembering to be the witness of your thoughts and feelings.
- Notice and try to accept things as they are, in the present moment – 'it is as it is' – without criticizing, condemning, judging, comparing or trying to change them.
- Continue your daily meditation, increasing the length of time by 5 minutes (up to 20 minutes) if and when you feel ready.
- Keep on with your 'mindfulness minutes' during the day, as often as you can.
- Be kind and loving to yourself: continue to notice and monitor your self-talk.

Week 3

What Causes Suffering?

nother week has passed and the entire group are here again. We're all back in our places, sitting quietly. There is a feeling of warmth, anticipation; the group seems happy to be together, pleased to be back. I wonder how they got on with their meditation – whether they managed to fit it in every day and how it's been going.

I know that Nikki is enjoying it because she told me so during a brief chat in the hall when she arrived. And I was correct, she does do yoga, but she did not stumble into the wrong group, as I had feared; she said she has wanted to learn about mindfulness meditation for a while.

The monk is right; being mindful is a question of practice. I have been finding that the more I do it, the easier it is, although I'm always like that at the beginning of a project: full of enthusiasm and optimism.

I suppose I am luckier than many of the members of the group in that I work from home – I am either in the kitchen, creating and testing recipes for my cookery books and articles, or at my desk writing them up. Or, doing my least favourite task – shopping in the supermarket for ingredients.

It's not the actual shopping I dislike. I enjoy looking at produce, especially fruit and vegetables, and unusual spices and flavourings – I get many of my ideas for recipes in this way. It's the pressure of being surrounded by crowds of people that I dislike and, more particularly, queuing.

Having said that, I realize how much I have been judging

everything. Thinking of queuing as my 'least favourite task' is 'labelling' something that is entirely neutral in itself, bestowing upon it characteristics that it doesn't really have. It's just queuing. It is as it is.

The monk looks around the group and smiles. 'So, how have you all been getting on?' he asks. 'I hope you are beginning to experience for yourselves the peace and strength that mindfulness and meditation can bring, and that you have been able to practise them and are feeling the benefit.'

There is the sound of affirmation from the group.

I must say, leaving aside the odd 'blip', I have been finding it really helpful. I wish that I had known about it years ago. It's strange, really, because I was brought up in the religious organization that my grandmother started and meditation was one of the key things we did there. But mindfulness was never mentioned. The meditation we did there at that time was the visualization-type. We sat quietly, listened to a piece of uplifting music, and the person conducting the group would describe a picture, usually a lotus on a still pool. Then we had to focus on that and any other images that unfolded from it.

It was peaceful and pleasant, but after I had done it for many years I felt very 'stuck' and reached a time when I thought to myself: *if I have to visualize another lotus pool I will throw something into it*. So although I was still in the organization at that time, I stopped listening to the voice of the person conducting the meditation, ceased visualizing anything when I meditated and just tried to find stillness in myself. I suppose my instinct was leading me towards mindfulness, even though I did not know anything about it at that time.

Had I been aware of mindfulness then, I think my life would have been different. As it was, I felt I was a failure – too out of tune with many of the things that they were doing at the retreat centre to belong there, and riddled with doubts and questions that I could not share with my family because all of them except Robert believed implicitly in the teaching. If I had not had the support and love of Robert, who was working in the organization with me and shared the same concerns, I do not know what I would have done.

In the end we moved away – one of the most challenging things I have ever done. It was difficult on many levels: physically, because we had no money (we had given everything we had to the retreat centre); mentally and spiritually, because I was in turmoil about whether I was doing a terrible thing in turning my back on 'the teaching' – would I be damned forever? I really did worry about that; and emotionally because all my family were still living and working there, still following all the teaching implicitly. And although I had some friends at the retreat centre, there were very, very few with whom I could share my agony of mind because most, like my family, would not hear anything against the teaching.

At that time, I did not know what I believed in – or whether I believed in anything at all. I shut right down. I remember thinking one day that I didn't believe I could feel any worse or any more depressed than I did at that moment. I felt as if I was sitting on the seabed and then I suddenly thought that at least if I was at the bottom of the world, I couldn't sink any further.

From that moment, I started to recreate my life. A friend recommended some workshops in transpersonal psychology and, through these, I was able to make sense of what was going on. Gradually, I rebuilt things. Some surprising events occurred that enabled Robert and me to buy a house and – perhaps the biggest miracle of all – I unexpectedly became pregnant with my third daughter, which was an incredible source of joy and healing for me and strangely symbolic of my emerging new life.

At the same time, I was making new friends and my cookery writing was taking off. I had some wonderful opportunities and was able to fit them in around my family life. Gradually I was getting back in touch with my spiritual side through the transpersonal work and also through reading some very helpful books, especially those of Wayne Dyer and Louise Hay, and later Leslie Kenton's *Journey to Freedom* and the books of Doreen Virtue.

The sound of the monk's voice brings me back to the present with a jump. Goodness, my mind is wandering all over the place! I must get a grip. I listen carefully to what he is saying.

'Do you have any questions about your meditation or about practising the First Noble Truth?

Joan, Rodney's wife, hesitates, then says, 'My mind is still very active most of the time. I do find it difficult to meditate for a full

20 minutes.' She pauses, and then says 'it's not just the thoughts, but sometimes I just find it really, well, *boring...*'

I know exactly what she means.

The monk laughs. 'Yes, it can be', he agrees. 'But if you're being truly mindful, when the whole of "this moment" fills your mind there is no room for boredom.'

The monk reflects then says. 'But if you are troubled by boredom – and I have to be honest, it's something we all face at some time when we're meditating – you can turn your mindfulness to the boredom. Examine it. What does it really feel like? What is the quality of boredom? Does it have a form? Keep breathing, keep being mindful of boredom, breathe into the boredom and you will find it passes. As I said before, when you are being truly mindful, you are never bored.

'Or, when you realize you're feeling bored, you could simply turn your mind to your breathing and focus on the in-breath and the out-breath, from the first intake of air into your body to the end of the exhalation. Your breath is always there for you; your breath is like your best friend.'

The monk pauses again, then Maggie says, 'May I ask what you think about pins-and-needles?' For a moment my mind goes blank and I feel as though I've strayed into a sewing class. 'Sometimes my legs go completely numb', she continues, 'and I panic in case I'll never get the feeling back in them. I just have to move.'

Ah, now I'm with her. I understand; I've had the same thing.

The monk smiles as he answers, 'A lot of odd physical

sensations can come up when you're meditating', he says. 'The best thing is not to make too much of them. Give them what we call "bare attention", just as you do with worrying thoughts or anything else that arises to distract you. The pins and needles will go of their own accord, as will the numbness. After you have been regularly meditating for a while, you won't get them any more. The body gradually adjusts. But be kind to it; sit as comfortably as you can and send some *metta* or loving kindness to any aches and pains.'

'Like I'm doing with the sadness that I have been feeling about my father?' asks Maggie.

'Yes', replies the monk, then adds, 'are you finding that it helps?'

'I am', confirms Maggie, 'just a little, but I am definitely noticing it.'

'Bit by bit it will improve', says the monk, 'or, as the Buddha said, "A jug fills drop by drop".'

Tim catches the monk's eye. He has a question to ask. 'When you suggest "sending *metta*" to painful legs or to sadness, can you explain a little more what you mean?'

'Yes', answers the monk. 'Suppose your legs are aching during your meditation practice – or at any other time, for that matter. First of all focus on the feeling of the pain. Be mindful of it. Experience it without judging or commenting on it. Hold it in your mind. Then bring into your mind the feeling of loving kindness toward your legs.'

This makes everyone laugh, including the monk.

'I know it sounds silly', explains the monk, 'but it works. So just think to yourself how much you appreciate your legs and feel a glow of warmth in your heart as you think about them. That's "sending *metta*". You can do it with any part of your body – with any thing or any person, come to that', he says.

The monk smiles. 'It's simple', he says, 'but it really works – "magic *metta*", I sometimes call it. It's another aspect of the Buddha's teaching that you can test out for yourselves.'

'Now, let's continue our study of the Noble Truths.

The monk pauses, looks around the group, then says: 'so let's quickly remind ourselves of what we've learned so far.

'We've considered the First Noble Truth, that "there is suffering, suffering should be understood, suffering has been understood". We have discovered that the way to find freedom from suffering is first to become an observer of the suffering, then to observe the suffering that we are feeling without commenting on it to ourselves or judging it – just letting it be. We know that it will go, we feel it lessening its grip, we let it slip away. Life gives us plenty of opportunities for putting this to the test and there's no doubt that it does work; it does bring happiness, freedom and peace.'

I agree. I have been trying this quite a bit. It's funny, because I am by nature an optimist – I definitely think my glass is half full rather than half empty – but I still worry a lot about little things, such as whether I'm going to miss a train, whether there will be enough money to pay the bills or whether my daughters are OK;

you know, the usual stuff.

When I have noticed that I'm worrying about something, I have been saying to myself, "there is suffering", and concentrating on "standing under" it – not blotting it out of my mind with a drink or a piece of chocolate or some other diversionary tactic. It's surprising to discover how many of these I find I have!

But it is equally surprising how, if you really do 'observe' a thought or a feeling without commenting on it or blaming yourself for having it in the first place or trying to make it go, it really does just disappear of its own accord. That has been another revelation for me.

'But', continues the monk, 'what if we could find the *cause* of our suffering? Wouldn't that help even more? How often do we ask ourselves '*Why* do we suffer? What is the *cause* of our suffering? We sometimes ask, "Why, why, why?" but do we look for the real cause of our suffering?

'We might think it's our difficult partner, the neighbours' loud music, an irritating dog barking, the bad economic climate, our stressful work situation, our arthritis or whatever. But do such things *really cause us to suffer*?

'Not according to the Buddha', he adds with a laugh. 'Having shown us how to focus on our suffering and decrease it by accepting it and letting it be, the Buddha then went on to give us the Second Noble Truth to help us find what caused the suffering in the first place.

'Like the First Noble Truth, it has three parts:

"There is the origin of suffering, which is the attachment
to desire.
Attachment to desire should be let go of.
Attachment to desire has been let go of."

There is the origin of suffering, which is attachment to desire

'We are told, 'the origin of suffering is attachment to desire' and the Buddha identified three kinds of desire:

- desire for sensual pleasure
- desire to become something
- desire to get rid of something

'Sometimes we shorten these to "greed, delusion and hatred" (or greed, hatred and delusion to put them in the order most people say them). But however you list them and whatever you call them, it's really all about wanting. It can be wanting or craving for something, or not wanting – detesting, hating – something, maybe so much that you want to get rid of it. It can be wanting to become something or 'delusion' – that is, wanting things to be different from what they are and not being satisfied with 'what is'. Or, to put it another way, it's all about attachment to desire: desire to have something; desire to change something; and desire not to have something – to get rid of it. We may experience more than one of these desires at once – for example, desire to get rid of something so that we can become something else.'

He's describing me, I think to myself. I'm always living my life in the future, wanting something or wanting to get rid of something so that I can become something better. For example, wanting to get rid of the extra pounds on my hips so that I can become slimmer and then, of course, naturally, happier. Yes, I have the desire to get rid of as well as the desire to become and for things to be different.

But the monk is continuing, 'However we name them and in whatever order we list them, I'm sure we can all recognize these cravings; they're part of being human. I remember when I was a novice in a monastery and at meal times had to stand far back in the queue. You'd be surprised how much you find you want that crisp, golden roast potato when it's the last one left and the monk in front of you takes it – and how much you can hate him for it!'

We laugh, many of us I'm sure, identifying cravings for certain things: smooth chocolate; crispy golden fries; a warm, flaky croissant; a cup of tea or coffee; a glass of wine. Surely this Noble Truth can't apply to those simple pleasures?

'But where's the in harm in fancying a delicious curry or some hot, crusty bread from the oven?' asks Pam, the tall woman with the short blonde bob.

'Do such thoughts make you suffer?' asks the monk. 'Simply thinking about things in a mild, happy way does not make for suffering. It might bring a vague feeling of sadness or dissatisfaction, of worry and of tension, but probably not much suffering.'

'But,' continues Pam, 'if I was fancying a takeaway and when I got to the shop it had just closed or the queue was too long, I'd be angry and probably want it even more.'

'You can't have it, so you really, really want it?' says the monk, laughing. Pam nods.

'So "fancying" has turned into "I absolutely must have, it's the one thing I want and I hate the shop or the long queue for stopping me from having it". Like me with the last roast potato...'

Pam smiles and the group laughs again.

The monk explains, 'No one is judging you for wanting, hating, being deluded. You are the one who knows when you are suffering. You know that mildly wanting something is quite different in terms of suffering, to desperately desiring something and not being able to have it. We've hit on the crux of the matter here. It's the *degree* of wanting or not wanting that makes the difference. It's the amount of emotional charge or, as it says in the second Noble Truth the "attachment" to the desire – the amount we want it, the strength of our wanting, the "craving and clinging", as the Buddha called it – that causes the suffering.

'When we love something or something makes us happy, we want it to continue or we want more of it. Then, if we can't have it or it's taken away from us, we suffer.

'So what can we do about it? Sometimes we can change the things around us. We may be able to replace something when it is broken: get a new car, a new job, a new partner even, but if we're looking to these to supply our happiness and peace of mind, we cannot rely on them because they will not stay as they are.

'The truth of the matter is *nothing stays the same*. Life is constantly changing and we never know what is going to happen. The Buddha referred to the changing quality of life as "impermanence". He noticed that whatever is born or created at some time ceases and, if we have become attached to it, we suffer.

'If we're lucky we might be able to get everything just as we want it: a perfect home, a perfect job, perfect relationships and a perfect income, but we can't freeze-frame these so that they stay the same. Our circumstances will change and if we're attached to them and they change in a way we don't like, we will suffer. That's life; that's why it's full of suffering.'

The monk pauses. 'But it doesn't have to be that way! We can't change life, but we can change ourselves and the way we look at things. We can free ourselves from suffering; we have the power within us. It takes practice and resolution, but it can be done.'

The monk stops again, then continues: 'I have experienced it in my own life. I used to be full of anger and insecurity and I went through bleak periods of dark depression. It took persistence to free myself, but I got there. It may be two and a half thousand years old, but the Buddha's method really does work.'

I look at the monk, sitting there, poised and smiling. He's radiating happiness, possessing nothing except his robe, shoes and the bowl from which he eats his two meals of the day. I wonder how long it takes to become so serene.

'It's all very well for a monk, though,' says Ed, 'living in a protected environment away from all the pressures of the world. I think it might be more difficult for those of us who have to go out to work to pay the mortgage, deal with tiresome bosses and work mates, and struggle to make ends meet and so on.'

This sounds a little rude to me, but the monk seems completely unfazed. 'Yes. Life is tough', he replies. 'Maybe this teaching is of even more value when you're out in the world – maybe. But I can assure you that going into a monastery is not an escape from problems. We don't have to pay the mortgage but, as part of a mendicant order, we do rely totally on gifts – or 'alms' – to keep going. They could dry up at any time.

'Going into a monastery doesn't mean we escape from ourselves, either. Long hours of meditation bring up all kinds of suffering states of mind and emotion that we have to deal with. And don't think that we get away from "tiresome bosses and work mates" either', he says, with a laugh.

'No, I don't really mean that,' he adds quickly. 'Let's just say that human nature is human nature and you don't get away from it just because you're in a monastery. It's natural to find some of the monks easier to get on with than others. In fact, because you're all together in a closed community, if you do not get on with someone, you can't get away – you just have to resolve the problem within yourself.

'But the nagging voice inside our head is not confined to monastics. I doubt there's anyone in the world who does not have it: it's all part of being a human being. Whether you're in a monastery or out in the world, life brings its pressures and challenges. Change happens; desires, cravings, clingings, attachments, hopes and wishes arise. We all get plenty of opportunities to put the Buddha's teaching into practice.

'Suffering can come from the attachment we have to ideas and ideals, as well as to more concrete things. As a monk it's easy to feel you are falling short of what you ought to be and think: *I should meditate more; I should be kinder and more considerate; I should work harder; I should be more punctual* and so on. The nagging internal voice goes on and on.

'And then we may try to fix the world: "It shouldn't be like this"; or we try and fix other people: "you really should be more tidy", and so on. This is all desire to become, maybe also mixed with desire to get rid of: *I should be kinder and more tolerant therefore I must get rid of my impatience.*

'We're into the "shoulds" and "oughts" again, says the monk. "Should, should, should; ought, ought, ought". Listen out for them; they're sure signs of some form of attachment going on; attachment to an ideal or an idea.'

When the monk says this, it reminds me of something I read some years ago in a book called *You Can Heal Your Life* by Louise

Hay, in which she notes how destructive those words, 'should', and 'ought' can be and suggests we 'bin' them – just stop using them. This idea really resonated with me and I did stop using them. So much so that when I heard the monk use the word 'should' in the Noble Truths – "suffering *should* be understood" etc, I found it really grated on me.

I'm reflecting on this – how liberating I found it to stop using these words and how over the years I've also had some struggles with copy editors who have added them to my manuscript as they edited my books – "this *should* be served piping hot"; "the oven *should* be preheated"; and so on, when the sound of the monk's voice brings me back into the present with a jump.

'"I want it to be this way and I don't want it to be that way"', he's saying. 'Desire makes us difficult to please – judging, comparing, criticizing, what we call in Buddhism "picking and choosing". But when you bring yourself into the present moment and get a sense of how you are feeling *now* as you gently breathe in and then let it go, you will be able to say to yourself "now, at this present moment, all is well"'.

The monk pauses for a moment, closes his eyes, and takes in a long, slow breath. I do the same and feel the tension in my body relaxing, the breath calming me.

The monk smiles, and chuckles a little. 'You know, what we have been saying about "picking and choosing" reminds me of a little story about the Buddha', he says. 'It's called the 84th problem – maybe some of you have heard it?'

No one speaks; the monk continues. 'It goes like this', he says. 'One day a farmer came to the Buddha because he was very burdened by all the problems in his life and he hoped that the Buddha might be able to help him.

'The Buddha listened patiently as the farmer related how his crops had failed, his wife's cooking was bad, his children were lazy, the rats were eating his eggs, the town was full of thieves, and so on and so on.

'Then the Buddha replied: "I am sorry, I cannot help you. Everyone has 83 problems. If you solve one problem, another one will surely take its place. And some problems, such as death, have no solution."

'The farmer was downcast. Then the Buddha said, 'But I can help you with the 84th problem.'

'What is that?' asked the farmer.

'Your desire to have no problems', replied the Buddha.

The monk laughs at his own joke, but we are quiet. 'Do you get it?' he asks, looking around the group. No one responds, so the monk explains, 'It's about attachment, isn't it? The farmer is *wanting* to have no problems; he's *craving*, *attached* to the desire for a problem-free life and that in itself is making him suffer. Resisting anything brings pain, whereas accepting and embracing things bring peace.'

The monk pauses, then adds, 'I sometimes think of that story when life seems to be full of problems and I find myself "picking and choosing" instead of accepting things as they are, now.

'But let's get back to the Second Noble Truth,' he continues. 'We've considered the first part, "there is the origin of suffering, which is the attachment to desire", and we've looked at the three types of desire: "greed, hatred and delusion" or "wanting, not wanting, and wanting things to be different", as identified by the Buddha. So if you are clear about that, let's move on to the second aspect of this Noble Truth:

Attachment to desire should be let go of

The monk pauses for a moment, then says: '"Desire should be let go of" ... yes, I know, there's the "s" word – "should" – that I've been advising you not to use!' he says with a laugh. 'But I think it's allowed in this instance. Judge for yourselves when you've heard me out.

'So', he repeats, 'desire should be let go of. If attachment to desire causes us to suffer, then to release ourselves from suffering, we have to let go of our attachment to desire. So how do we do that?

'The first step, as we found in the First Noble Truth, is to be aware of what is happening within us. In the First Noble Truth we got into "observer mode" and recognized "there is suffering"; we concentrated on that suffering; we let it be and we let it go.

'Now, with the Second Noble Truth, we have more insight into *why* we are suffering so, as we get into "observer mode" and view the suffering – notice I said *the* suffering, not "our" suffering – we can see that it is caused by, well, let's not beat about the bush here: greed, hatred or delusion, clinging and craving.

'The moment you can view the suffering like this, you loosen its hold over you. You see it for what it is and then you can begin to let it go. You can move on to the second part of the Second Noble Truth: "desire should be let go of".

'So how do you let go of things? When you find yourself attached, the first thing to do is exactly what we have been doing with the First Noble Truth – view what is happening. You think: *That longing I've got for the new car – better job, slimmer body, more money, latest fashion, (you fill in the words) – is an attachment to desire.*

'Or it might be that you have a loathing toward the government, paying taxes, "lazy people" or whatever is annoying you. Instead of venting your spleen on others or the situation, say to yourself: "ah, there is suffering" or "that's attachment to hatred, or maybe a mixture of hatred and delusion", because you hate the situation as it is and want it to be different.

'Whatever the situation or the feeling that is causing you pain, once you recognize it for what it is: attachment to one type of desire or another, or a mixture, there's a sense of relief. It's as if the tension goes and you sigh and relax a bit. It's what they call an "aha!" moment.

I Met a Monk

'Then you don't go on digging away at it; *you let it be*. And when you do so, its hold on you will loosen even more. Eventually – or even immediately, once you really get into the habit of this – it will go. It will dissolve like snow in the sunshine; your heart will open and you'll be free. Oh, it's such a lovely feeling of relief and spaciousness as the clinging and craving dissolve.'

The monk stops for a moment, his eyes closed and a smile on his face, as if he's really feeling it. Then he continues thoughtfully, 'When you're letting go of attachments, remember that "letting go" is not "getting rid of" or "throwing away". Think about it – the urge *to get rid of* is another desire, so to try and let go of craving by getting rid of it is simply layering one desire on top of another. Letting go is different from getting rid of. Letting go means putting down, setting aside.

'Jack Kornfield, who trained as a Buddhist monk and is now a respected teacher of meditation in America, put it in a succinct and memorable way:

"Letting go is not
Getting rid of
Letting go is
Letting be."

The monk pauses and looks around the group. 'Do you understand this?' he asks. We're all very silent, trying to get our heads around this concept of letting go. He picks up his glass of water to demonstrate. 'Look, I'm holding this glass – grasping this glass – and I want to let go of it. I don't have to throw it in the rubbish bin to do that. I can simply put it down', he says, placing it on the tray beside him.

'That's what we do with all our attachments. It's not the attachment that's the problem, it's the holding on to it. So what do we do? We recognize the desire or attachment without judging it. We might think about wanting to get rid of it because we don't want to have this desire – but what we do is just lay it aside, as I did with the glass. And to do this, we view our suffering from our "observer" position. We see it for what it is: greed, hatred and delusion, clinging and craving. We think, *ah, yes, that's what it is* and realize we're no longer attached to it. We let it go.

'You see, once we look at and listen to our desires, we are no longer attached to them: we're viewing them and allowing them to be the way they are. Then we realize we can lay them aside and let them go.

'At first this letting go may only be this much', says the monk, holding up his forefinger and thumb just the tiniest fraction apart. 'And the feeling of letting go might be tiny; it might be just a flash of "letting go" and then the craving, hate, delusion or whatever it is, comes back.

'But keep doing it: a second of "letting go" here, another a tiny bit longer, there; it builds up and soon you'll find you've let go for a little bit longer – a minute, several minutes or more. It's a bit like swimming or riding a bike or learning any new technique. At first you can just do it for a moment, but as you practise you find you can do it for longer and longer, until it becomes so natural that you can't imagine not being able to do it; it really becomes a way of life.

Attachment to desire has been let go of

'How will I know when I've done that?' asks Nikki.

'You will know. But don't worry about it. Just keep letting the suffering or the desire, be. Accept it as it is. Don't judge it. And don't judge yourself for having it – as we said with the First Noble Truth, accept it as it is. Let it be. Allow it. Say "welcome" to it, send it *metta* or loving kindness. Simply accept it for what it is: *Oh, that's a craving for success, that's what it is.* And let it be'.

'You'll feel it release its grip on you for an instant and that will be the beginning of letting go. Every time you're aware of feeling it, repeat this process of letting it be. Gradually, as I said, you'll be able to let it be for longer and longer. And then one day you'll realize the emotional charge has gone; the craving no longer has you in its grip – you will have let it go and you will be free.

'Letting go is like anything else. The more you do it, the more you'll see how to do it. The more you practise it, the easier and more natural it will become and the longer you will be able to sustain the beautiful state of non-attachment.'

'But how can I be *sure* I've let go', Sam asks, looking serious and frowning slightly.

The monk pauses. He closes his eyes, takes a deep breath and then speaks again. 'You'll know that you've let go of desire when you no longer try to get rid of anything but recognize it just the way it is; when you no longer judge; when you are peaceful and calm, accepting people and situations exactly as they are, without any urge to condemn, compare or criticize anyone, or anything, even yourself. Then you'll know true peace, freedom and well-being. And, I can tell you, that that is the most glorious feeling.'

'Just knowing things as they are in the present moment, and allowing them to be exactly as they are, without feeling the necessity to change them or to pass judgment upon them – that is true freedom and joy. And once you've found it, it just increases and increases. You'll see ...'

The monk stops speaking. There is a most beautiful atmosphere in the room; it almost feels as though the room has expanded and is full of golden light. For a flash I get a sense of the state of bliss that the monk is talking about.

After some moments of this, the monk gives a little chuckle, and says, 'There's rather a nice Buddhist story about letting go. Would you like to hear it?'

There is a muttering of affirmation from the group.

'Some of you may know it already', says the monk, 'as it's quite a famous story, but I think it's worth repeating because it holds a wise message for us all.

'It goes like this. A senior and a junior monk are travelling together. They come to a river with a strong current. A pretty young woman is walking along the riverbank looking very upset.

"What is the matter?" asks the senior monk.

"'I'm really worried", replies the girl, "because my father is ill and I need to cross the river in order to get to him but the bridge has collapsed. Do you know where the next bridge is?"

"Oh, it's miles away", replies the monk. "But don't worry; I can carry you over the water".

'The girl gratefully accepts the offer of help and the senior monk carries her on his back to the other side of the river, puts her down and says goodbye.

'The junior monk is very troubled by what has happened. He knows that monks are not allowed to touch women and he is furious and upset that the senior monk has broken his vows. He continues to fume and agonize over this for some time. Finally, he can bear it no longer and he confronts the senior monk.

'When he hears what is upsetting the young student so much, he bursts out laughing. "Goodness", he says, "I put that woman down when we reached the other side of the river. Are you still carrying her?"

'This little story reminds us about letting go of attachments and putting them down, not continuing to carry them. It is also instructive in that it demonstrates that when we follow our heart – not our "desire", but our true, deep instinct that always points us toward the real essence of Buddhism, which is loving kindness – we may sometimes have to break a rule.

'But what is the right thing to do: break a rule in order to perform an act of loving kindness to a stranger in distress or follow the rule book and let them suffer? Follow that deep inner voice – that sense of love – or listen to the nagging "should" and "ought" voice, which comes from our fearful inner critic?

'This is something we'll think about further when we consider the Fourth Noble Truth, which is all about putting this teaching into practice in our everyday lives – taking it off the meditation mat and into the market place.'

The monk looks around the group and smiles. 'Well, there's been quite a lot to take in this afternoon.' He looks out into the garden, green and inviting, a perfect summer afternoon.

'Why don't we refresh ourselves now with a walking meditation outside?' he suggests. 'The Buddha thought very highly of walking meditation. It's a way of bringing mindfulness right into our daily life; something we can do every day.

'In fact', continues the monk, 'once you get used to it you can do a walking meditation almost anywhere, at any time. It's like breathing. I like to say, "if you can breathe, you can meditate"; and you can also say, "if you can walk, you can meditate"'.

I like the sound of that. Something that appeals to me very much is the Buddha's practicality – how he has given us a method of meditation that doesn't require us to sit in golden temples or withdraw from the world, but that we can do as we go about our daily life.

'So', continues the monk, 'the clue really is in the name – a walking meditation is a meditation that you do when you're walking – and it's a most useful tool to have, as it's a wonderful way of calming and refreshing yourself.'

Walking Meditation

'Find a space where you can walk forward in a straight line and then back again. You can choose the number of paces – ten, twenty, thirty or whatever feels comfortable, but you don't need to count them constantly.

'Stand still for a moment or two before you begin; check that your head is straight – neither pointing up nor down – and your chin is slightly tucked in.

'Let your arms rest by your side or, if you prefer, try clasping your hands in front of you, and keep a slight tension in them because this makes you more attentive.

'Look about two metres (six feet) in front of you; soften your gaze.

'Take a few mindful breaths, counting in your usual way, if that is what you do. Then walk in a steady but natural way, pausing at the end for a moment or two before turning round and walking back.

'Keep your mind totally on the present moment, as you do in your meditation. Notice how you are feeling. Experience the feeling of the ground under your feet, the sun and the slight breeze on your face, the sound of the birds, the scent of the flowers or any other sensations.

'When your mind wanders (as it will, because that is its nature), simply notice it, stand still and bring it back to the present moment, to the ground under your feet.

'Then continue to walk and notice the steadiness of your paces.

'If little worries or irritations creep in, let them be and just gently return to watching your breath.

'Find a mode and a rhythm that feels natural. Be present. Be purposeful. Be mindful. Be aware of your body and your breath.'

We walk out into the garden. The birds are singing and the air feels warm on my face. I compose myself, take a deep, gentle breath and start to walk steadily and purposefully.

We have removed our shoes, as is Buddhist practice, and I love the feeling of the grass beneath my bare feet. I find this decidedly relaxing and pleasant, though I am surprised to find how wobbly my ankles are when I'm walking this slowly.

Although we have a fair-sized garden, it is overlooked by several houses and I find myself wondering what the neighbours will think if they see a motley group of people and a monk walking backward and forward in straight lines. I feel sure they would laugh at us, and for a moment I feel embarrassed and mortified at the thought, and wonder what I will say to them.

Then I catch myself. I remember the monk's words about just bringing our mind gently back to the present when we find it has wandered. I take a deep breath and feel the air going down inside me – calming, refreshing. The steady rhythm of my walking and the feeling of the ground beneath my feet calm me. I feel centred, strong, peaceful.

My thoughts return to how ridiculous we must all look walking up and down the garden and I feel uncomfortable again. Is anyone watching us? Are they laughing? What *will* the neighbours think?

I bring my consciousness back again to my original feeling of discomfort, of embarrassment, of being "different" from other people. A memory from my early childhood comes into my head. I remember sensing from my mother her unvoiced fears that I would find it difficult to make friends because I was a bit different from other children. (Who else in the 1950s had a mother who was an astrologer? And a grandmother who was a spirit medium channelling a Native North American and running a retreat centre?)

I always felt a pressure to 'make friends' in order to please my mother, but it wasn't easy because I also sensed, from a young age and without being told, that it was wise to keep my mouth well closed about pretty much anything to do with my family life. As a result, I could never be completely open with any friends that I did make, as their lives were so different from my own. I lived in a secluded place with no car, where 'strange' activities (like meditation), séances and secret meetings went on.

Admitting to being vegetarian was strange enough in those days, though I was passionate about it as it was my choice from a very early age. For some reason I never found it difficult to explain: we just didn't eat fish or animals and that was that. Seemed perfectly reasonable to me (and still does!).

I became skilled at getting others to talk about themselves rather than revealing anything about myself. So I had this inner conflict: feeling I 'ought' to make friends in order to be an acceptable person in my mother's eyes, and yet not feeling comfortable about revealing anything about myself or committing to the intimacy that would allow me to get close to anyone.

Suddenly, as I'm musing on this, my mind comes back to the present moment and I realize how far my thoughts have wandered from the initial feeling of discomfort at potentially being spotted by my neighbours, to my childhood and being 'anti-social'. I now understand what the monk meant when he said that it's very easy to get pulled away from the initial feeling into a web of thoughts and issues.

Oh dear, I think, *I've got a long way to go on this path to perfect peace.* I'm still reflecting on all of this when I hear the gong that reminds us to return to the meditation room.

We walk back inside, smiling and refreshed. The monk is already in his place, sitting serene and tranquil like a statue of the Buddha. He smiles around at the group when we are settled in our places.

'So how was that?' he asks.

There are murmurs of positive appreciation.

'I enjoyed that', comments Robert. 'It always surprises me how refreshing a walking meditation can be.'

'May I ask a question?' asks Dan.

The monk nods and smiles.

'I'm struggling a bit with the idea of doing a walking meditation as I go about my normal life. Isn't it a bit dangerous? And what if I meet someone I know and they want to talk? They might think I'm being unfriendly if I just walk on, or that I've gone a bit bonkers or something. In fact, I think some of them think that already, with me taking up meditation', he says with a little laugh.

'You don't have to do it if you feel uncomfortable about it', replies the monk, 'but many people find that meditating when walking is a very practical and beneficial thing to do. Of course, you have to pick your place sensibly and maintain your awareness of both your walking and your whereabouts – but that's just good practice at being mindful.

'If you meet someone, you can break off your meditation at any time, greet them mindfully and then continue. Or you could just say, "sorry I can't talk now, I'm doing a walking meditation", and continue. You can always explain more later – you never know, they might start doing it themselves.

'Is it better to do a sitting meditation or a walking meditation?' asks Ed.

'They are both helpful', replies the monk. 'Some people find walking meditation easier to do than sitting, but they both bring results. In the monastery we alternate walking meditations with sitting meditations.

'I recommend that you fit in a walking meditation each day if you can, even if it's just as you're walking to the station or the post box, walking the dog, or going to the shops – you can even do it walking upstairs. Try to do one sitting meditation and one walking meditation daily, if that is possible, but if you can only manage one, then make it a sitting meditation.'

'Thank you', says Dan.

'A daily walking meditation also gives you a very good opportunity to practise your *metta*', says the monk. As you walk, say the *metta* mantra to yourself: "May I be well. May I be happy. May I be safe and at ease". Try it for yourselves.'

The monk looks around the group and smiles. 'So, on that note of *metta*, why don't we join together in our closing chant', he says.

We move and there is the rustle of paper as we pick up our chanting sheets. The monk chants '*Araham*', and we join with him chanting '*sammasambuddho bhagava, Buddham bhagavantam abhivademi*', which means we 'render homage to the Buddha'. We bow.

'*Svakkhato*' – 'the teaching' – sings the monk and we join him with '*bhagavata dhammo, dhammam namassami*' – 'I bow to the teaching' – and we bow again.

Then '*Supatipanno*' – 'the Buddha's disciples' – chants the monk, and we join him with, '*bhagavato savakasangho, Sangham namami*' – 'I bow to all who have practised the teaching and brought it to us down the ages'.

We pause for a few moments to enjoy the feeling of peace and love that the chant has brought us, then we pick up our things and go our separate ways.

Quick Review

- Suffering is caused by attachment to desire: wanting, not wanting, wanting things to be different – 'greed, hatred and delusion, clinging and craving' as the Buddha said.
- Life is constantly changing, so becoming too attached to anything is setting ourselves up for suffering.
- We can enjoy life to the full by not depending on anything for our happiness, nor blaming anything for our pain.
- To free yourself from suffering:
  - Get into your 'observer' mode.
  - View what is happening.
  - Recognize it for what it is – attachment to one type of desire or another, or a mixture.
  - Let it be.
  - Let it go.

Practice

- Notice your suffering. Feel it; allow it to be. See if you can trace it back to an 'attachment' of some kind: wanting something, not wanting something, wanting things to be different. Let go the 'attachment', and feel the suffering lessen and begin to melt away.
- Listen to your thought and speech: 'shoulds' and 'oughts' are sure signs of some form of attachment – attachment to an ideal or an idea. Notice them and let them go.

- Continue your daily meditation for 15 to 20 minutes each day as well as practising 'mindfulness minutes' throughout the day as often as you can. Perhaps try a walking meditation.
- Spend a minute or two at the end of your meditation, whether you're walking or sitting, saying to yourself the *metta* words: 'May I be well. May I be happy. May I be safe and at ease'. Feel the tension go, feel peace fill your body.

Week 4
Finding Freedom

W e're sitting quietly, waiting for the monk to speak and I am reflecting on an incident that happened during the past week.

I had been practising hard with mindfulness meditation and observing my reactions to little things in my life – noticing 'there is suffering' when I have been upset, and tracing the cause back to being 'attached' to some idea or desire, or to some 'hate'. And I tried to let whatever it was 'be' without being critical of myself and then feel it go.

I was pleased with the way it had been going and the new sense of inner peace and strength that I had been experiencing. Then, one evening during the week I was in the car with Robert on the way to a meeting and I suddenly remembered I'd forgotten the milk that I was supposed to take. We were rather short of time, but he stopped at a supermarket and waited in the car park while I rushed in to get the milk.

I'd never been in that particular supermarket before. I felt anxious because I knew we were in a rush and I couldn't find the milk. I found it eventually, quickly picked up a bottle in my hand – no time for a basket – and hurried to the checkouts.

When I got there I was amazed and appalled to find there was only one open and no self-service checkouts at all. And there were about twenty people ahead of me. I looked around with disbelief. It was 7 o'clock in the evening – how could they only have one till open? I decided I hadn't got time to wait. I voiced my feelings loudly to the world around me, marched back to where

I'd got the milk from and angrily put it back. I walked furiously back to the car, almost tripping over on the way.

I got back into the car and noticed the surprised look on Robert's face, which seemed to be asking where the new calm woman he'd been living with since we started the Buddhism course had disappeared to – and, too late, I remembered mindfulness. I felt really mad at myself and disappointed. Then I realized that by feeling angry, disappointed and 'a failure' I was simply adding other layers of emotion to the situation.

I was so out of sorts that I didn't even try to notice my breathing. But at least I was aware of what had happened – and that certainly indicated some progress, if you can call it that. Not that Buddhists think in terms of 'progress': you don't, of course, when you're truly in the present moment. It's all 'now'.

In spite of that little blip, I have been continuing with my mindfulness practice, being in the present as often as I remember. Being mindful is becoming more normal for me, though there are many times when I forget and I still find it difficult to meditate for more than about 15 minutes at a time.

Most of the time meditation or mindfulness is for me more of a moment-to-moment experience – I'll be doing or thinking about something and I'll suddenly remember mindfulness. Then I'll bring my mind right into the present moment and notice my thoughts and how I am feeling, being careful not to judge or criticize them, of course – just observing, letting be and letting go.

I'm just reflecting on all of this when the monk's voice breaks into my thoughts.

'What a great group this is', he is saying, smiling. 'It's good to be back with you again. I'm so enjoying my time with you exploring the Noble Truths.'

He looks around at everyone and smiles.

'So, we have considered the first two Noble Truths, and now we have come to the third. Let us have a quick recap so we can see how they all fit together.

'With the First Noble Truth we learned about the presence of suffering and how to view it dispassionately, not as a part of us but as a condition passing through. We learned to become the observer, to watch the suffering within us and to let it be and, by doing this, allow it to dissipate of its own accord.'

The monk continues, 'Then, in the Second Noble Truth we considered the *cause* of suffering, which is attachment to desire – greed, hate, delusion, clinging and craving– so that when we suffer, we can understand what is going on. We notice not simply the pain, but also the arising of the attachments and the cravings that cause the pain. Once again, we learn to watch them, let them be and let them go.

'When we become really practised at this, we can notice the beginning of a clinging, a delusion and a craving, and nip it in the bud by letting it go before it gets strong enough to disrupt our peace and cause us to suffer.

'So now we come to the Third Noble Truth, which is this:

"There is the cessation of suffering.
The cessation of suffering should be realized.
The cessation of suffering has been realized."'

I find this confusing. The monk looks at me, notices my puzzlement and asks, 'Do you have a question about this?'

I reply, 'Yes, I am a bit surprised because I thought that letting go of attachment to desire, as we learned in the Second Noble Truth, meant the end of suffering. But now you are telling us that the Third Noble Truth is about "the cessation of suffering". So how does the Third Noble Truth differ from the Second Noble Truth?'

'Ah', says the monk, 'although the Four Noble Truths are listed numerically, they are really all aspects of the same truth – that there is suffering and that we have within us the power to end suffering – and in practice they overlap, working together, complementing each other. You see, you need the four wheels of your car all turning in order to get you to your destination,' he adds, with a little laugh.

'As we go about our life practising the first two Noble Truths: noticing, observing, being mindful, letting be and letting go, we find we become much more accepting of the whole of life. All that is in the present moment – 'the good, the bad and the ugly' to quote the Clint Eastwood film – we realize is all part of life, all part of "now".

'It is all happening now, at the present moment, and as such, if we want to be truly "present" and really part of the flow of life, we have to accept it – everything – as it is. It is as it is, there's no point in resisting. When we resist, we simply block the flow. It's as if instead of flowing *with* the stream of life, we're bumping up against the rocks, clinging to the reeds, trying to resist it or even to swim against it.

'As we learn to accept the present moment exactly as it is, we find that the desire to resist what is and to judge, criticize, condemn and compare, gradually lessens and we feel freer, more at peace. We flow.

'And, as we observe what is going on inside us – or, indeed, around us – and we learn to "let it be" and then "let it go", a remarkable thing happens. We notice that the suffering begins to ease. We stop bumping up against the rocks in the river. The clouds in the sky disappear, the sun comes out and we see it shine. We begin to experience the Third Noble Truth: "there is cessation of suffering."

'This may take time. At first it may be just a second of letting go here, another second there, then a minute, then a couple of minutes. Hour by hour, day by day, it builds up, until suddenly one day we realize that we haven't thought about that particular suffering all day: suffering has ceased.'

This really resonates with me. My mind goes back to when my father died, very suddenly, some years ago now. I was grief-stricken. It seemed as though I was in pain all day, every day. And every night I had sad dreams that he was going to die or that he had died. Day or night, I just couldn't get away from the grief.

I remember this went on for a whole month and then gradually the dreams receded and I only had them every other day, then just twice a week. And one day I was surprised to realize that I hadn't thought about him and wept all day! From then on the pain became less and less.

The sound of the monk's voice brings me back to the present moment.

'This is a normal healing process', he's saying, 'in which, instead of resisting, resenting or repressing the pain, we allow ourselves to feel it and accept it – or, even welcome and embrace it – in other words, we let it be.'

The monk pauses. Maggie catches his eye.

'Did you want to say something?' asks the monk.

'What you are saying', replies Maggie, 'about not resisting the pain and what you told me before about not being afraid of being overwhelmed by grief at the loss of my father but allowing myself to really feel the pain, is certainly helping me.'

'I am glad', says the monk. 'And that is what happens. When we accept the pain and refrain from commenting on it or from criticizing ourselves for having it, or telling ourselves we should be over it by now; when we just accept it – that's the start of the healing process. And gradually, little by little, we experience a cessation of suffering. We begin to understand for ourselves the meaning of the Third Noble Truth.

There is cessation of suffering

'The thing with the Four Noble Truths, and indeed with all the teaching of the Buddha as I've said before, is that it's experiential.

'The Buddha points the way, he tells us clearly what to do: how to free ourselves from suffering, how to find happiness; how to play our part in creating a beautiful world of peace and love. But it's up to us to actually do it. It's grown-up teaching; the Buddha treats us like adults, not children.

'There's no authority telling us what to do or criticizing us if we fall short, condemning us if we slip up. After all', he adds with a smile, 'who needs anyone else to do that when the inner voice in our head is quite capable of doing it for us?'

The group laughs.

'Now', he says, looking round the room, 'there is something that will help you to understand the Third Noble Truth, and indeed, all the Noble Truths. It is this insight that the Buddha gave his followers, "All that is subject to arising is subject to ceasing."'

There is silence as we try to get our heads around the significance of his words. '"All that is subject to arising is subject to ceasing"', he repeats. 'This is a universal truth. Everything in this world that arises or begins, also ceases, ends, is no more.'

I smile because the monk is reminding me of the dead parrot sketch in the Monty Python show of the 1970s: 'He's not pining, he's passed on. This parrot is no more. He has ceased to be. He's expired and gone to meet his maker. He's a stiff. Bereft of life, he rests in peace. If you hadn't have nailed him to the perch, he'd be pushing up the daisies. He's rung down the curtain and joined the choir invisible. This is an ex-parrot!'

I pull myself together and hear, '… our planet Earth, even the universe itself, they will eventually end.

'Think about it. Isn't life a series of beginnings and endings? We're born, we die; our bodies are changing every moment; our hair grows, our skin and the cells of our body renew themselves.'

'Don't they say that within a seven-year cycle every single cell of the body is replaced with a new one?' asks Gwyn.

'Yes, I have heard that', replies the monk. 'When we think about life: we grow up, go to school, finish school, go on to higher studies or work. We make friends, lose friends, find love, lose love. We may become parents and see the stages of life repeating themselves in a new generation. The only thing we can be sure of is change or "impermanence", as Buddhists often call it.

'The statement, "all that is subject to arising is subject to ceasing" applies to our pleasures in life, too, as well as to our thoughts and feelings, all physical life – everything. So, if we get attached to anything in this physical world, if we cling to anything, we know that we will suffer eventually because it will change or cease.

'But we don't have to suffer and we don't have to wait until we die for suffering to end. If we understand and put into practice the Four Noble Truths we can be free and happy *now*. This is the Buddha's great gift to us: freedom from suffering.

I'm pondering on all of this when Pam speaks up.

'That's all very well' she says, 'I can understand that if we don't get attached to things we don't get hurt. That reminds me of one of my boyfriends, Quentin, who was so scared of getting emotionally involved that he didn't allow himself to feel any emotion. If we go through life being afraid of getting attached to anything because we may get hurt when they disappear, where's the love and the joy in that?'

'Yes', agrees Suzi, we've all had a Quentin in our lives.'

'Too true', adds Joan and all the women in the group laugh, but the monk is serious. He pauses for a moment before resuming speaking.

'I understand what you are saying', he says. 'Many people struggle with getting this balance between head and heart, especially when they have been hurt in early life. The self-protective mechanism is to shut down the feeling part of our nature – it's safer to keep the heart closed than to risk being hurt by opening it to love.

'Keeping your heart open and loving while not getting attached is a delicate balance to achieve. When you love, you open yourself to the risk of being hurt. What is it they say, "Pain is the price you pay for love"? There's a lot of truth in that.

'But what we're learning to do is to appreciate something fully – even to relish it, to enjoy it in the moment – *but not to cling to it* – "to care and not to care", as T S Eliot put it. To enjoy the fragrance of a rose without wanting to pick it; the song of a nightingale without wanting to cage it; the sight of a butterfly fluttering on its rainbow wings without wanting to catch it; the love of another human being without wanting to possess them, and so on.

'We can't take our possessions with us when we die, and we certainly don't own anyone. Kalil Gibran put this so beautifully in his poem, *The Prophet*:

"Love one another, but make not a bond of love;

Let it rather be a moving sea between the shores of your souls.

Fill each other's cup but drink not from one cup."

'Oh yes, I love those words', I can't help saying. 'I discovered *The Prophet* when I was going through difficult times trying to disentangle myself from my very loving but extremely possessive parents. Kalil Gibran's words about parents and children really helped me, too, and have remained with me ever since:

"Your children are not your children.

They are the sons and daughters of Life's longing for itself.

They come through you but not from you.

And though they are with you yet they belong not to you.

You may give them your love but not your thoughts,

For they have their own thoughts.

You may house their bodies but not their souls,

For their souls dwell in the house of tomorrow,

which you cannot visit, not even in your dreams.

You may strive to be like them,

But seek not to make them like you.

For life goes not backward nor tarries with yesterday."

I stop, rather shocked and surprised at myself at getting so carried away. Robert catches my eyes and smiles at me: he knows how much those words mean to me. The group claps and I feel myself blushing, but the monk smiles widely.

'Quite so', he says with a chuckle. 'Quite so. Wise words, indeed. When we cling to, or get attached to anything in this physical world, whether it's our lover, our children, the latest mobile phone, our pet, our parents, our income, our life-style, our favourite kind of bread, a restaurant we love to go to, our car, that holiday we've looked forward to for so long; we know that it is subject to change – and eventually, cessation. "That which arises, ceases."

We are all very quiet, thinking about the monk's words. Then he continues. 'We know that life changes, our pleasures disappear. We also know from the Buddha's teaching that when we become mindful, when we notice our suffering, notice the attachment to desire that is causing it and then lay aside this desire instead of grasping it, the suffering ceases. Yes, truly, this does happen. The second insight into the Third Noble Truth tells us this.'

The cessation of suffering should be realized

'You just need to *do* it! The Buddha has told us clearly how to do it, step by step, but we have to do it for ourselves – and we can!'

The monk pauses, thoughtfully, then smiles, and adds, 'The Buddha also said, "there are only two mistakes one can make along the road to truth: not going all the way and not starting".

Don't let's make those mistakes and miss out on that peace and bliss that can be ours.

'So, we put into practice these Noble Truths in our everyday life and we find that our attachments and cravings are getting less and beginning to cease. This happens, we can all experience it for ourselves. It may be for only very brief periods of time – maybe for a second or two at first – but we notice it. We know that it is happening and we know when suffering has ceased.'

There is a pause, then Maggie asks, 'You mean like the pain I was feeling about my father's death?'

'Yes', answers the monk. 'It applies to all forms of suffering. As we practise mindfulness and we investigate what *causes* the suffering in the first place – passion, greed, hatred and delusion or greed, aversion and ignorance, however you like to word them – and let go of these, what we are left with is true freedom, peace and bliss, as we can all discover for ourselves.

'The Buddha likened these causes of suffering – the greed, hatred and delusion – to "fires" that burn us, and he said that the process of letting the suffering go was like "blowing out the fires". And the Pali word for blowing out is *nibbana* or *nirvana*, the state of pure peace, freedom and bliss that we are left with when the "fires" have been extinguished.'

The monk stops for a moment, thinking, then continues. 'So', he says, 'by experiencing everything that arises eventually ceases – desires, physical possessions, the seasons, nature, flowers, animals, human beings, loved ones, and so on – and by letting go of our attachments to them through our practice of mindfulness and the first two Noble Truths, we begin to experience the Third Noble Truth, "the cessation of suffering". Where the suffering was, we can instead find peace – a sense of freedom and "spaciousness" inside us.'

The monk pauses again. We are all completely silent. He continues, 'And as we focus on this peace in our mindfulness practice, we can begin to touch that part of our being that never changes, that strength and peace that just "is"; it doesn't arise, so it doesn't cease; it's always there. That's why in Buddhism we call it "the deathless".

There is another pause, then Gwyn asks, 'So what is it? What are we touching?'

'Let's see if we can identify it further', replies the monk. After a moment, he says, 'When we think about ourselves deeply, who and what are we? We are not our physical body, because that will die. We are no longer the baby, the schoolboy or -girl. Those days have passed.

'Nor are we our career persona: the teacher, the hairdresser, the monk, the doctor, the parent, the carer, the cookery writer', he says, looking at me. 'All those things that we become in our life have arisen; we pass through them and move on.'

Everyone is very quiet and thoughtful. Maybe, like me, they are reflecting a little on their past.

The monk continues, 'Neither are we our thoughts or our feelings because they arise and cease. And we are not our nationality, our beliefs, our views and prejudices, our religious denomination or any of the labels that we, or other people, put on us.'

The monk pauses again. 'So who are we really?' asks Rodney.

'All the things I have mentioned', says the monk, 'are what we have acquired as part of our conditioning, our education and our upbringing, and they can change.

'Do you mean they are what is sometimes called our ego?' asks Pam.

'Yes', replies the monk. 'Those are the things that make up what we call our "ego" or our "personality view", as the Buddha described it. To find out who we really are, we have to get beyond that, beyond the meaninglessness of titles such as "man", "woman", "Buddhist", "English", "Indian", "American" or any other nationality; or descriptions such as "pretty", "clever", "successful" or "stupid", "hopeless", "useless". Such terms just imprison us, especially when we experience them from our inner critic.'

'Labels we give ourselves, and others?' asks Pam.

'Yes', replies the monk. 'And they may engender fear, pride or separation from others whom we feel the need to criticize, put down or even fight in order to prove ourselves right, validate our views or make ourselves seem secure and successful.'

'The Buddha described the ego – this "personality-view" – as a kind of structure that we build around ourselves like a house from the time we are very, very young, to protect ourselves from hurt and harm.

'It is our view of ourselves. For example, I'm a man, a Theravada Buddhist monk who has practised in the monastery and become an *ajahn* or "teacher". So I have attained some success, some standing in the group, which makes me feel pleased and maybe a bit, superior. All that is ego – the house I've built around myself to make me feel comfortable and secure.'

The group laughs a little and the monk continues, 'We all do it', he says, 'we all create this shelter, this place of apparent safety to stop ourselves from being hurt. And it can and does do this. But it also traps us. If we shut ourselves up inside our protective shelter, we can't get out. We lose our freedom and we get cut off and separated from other people – separated from who we really are, the true being or presence that is deep within us behind "the man", "the woman", "the monk" and so on.'

The monk looks around the group. We're all silent, listening intently.

'So', he says at last, 'we've looked at what we're not, but to get back to your question, Rodney, of what or who we are really … Let's pause for a moment and examine it to see if we can find out for ourselves. Let's share a few moments of mindfulness.'

The monk breathes deeply; the group moves a little to get comfortable and people sit up straight.

'Straighten your spine', says the monk. 'Close your eyes. Notice your breathing – take a few breaths.'

There is silence for a minute or two. 'Now', says the monk, 'Breathe in and ask yourself "who am I?" 'Listen inwardly. Notice the pause that follows that question. Keep your attention on that pause, that emptiness and see how long you can hold it without any thoughts coming in. When you notice your mind coming back, ask yourself again, "who am I?" and notice, even "listen" to the pause that follows.

'When you concentrate on that, where is the sense of self, of "I"? You know that you "the man" or you "the woman", you "the doctor" or you "the cookery writer" are not there. There's just emptiness – as one Buddhist teacher put it "just vast emptiness". There's no "me" or "mine" there; just space, purity, alertness, attention.

'In emptiness we are just what we are. At this moment, when we experience this emptiness, this consciousness, everything is as it is. Everything is just the way it's supposed to be. We can drop the burdens from our shoulders because we can see that "it is as it is" and there is no person there to be involved or to do or be anything.

'For a moment we have opened the door of our ego house a crack. We have experienced a sense of spaciousness and clarity; we have touched an inner sense of safety and well-being that far transcends any safety our house can bring us

'In emptiness things are just what they are. When we are in this space, it doesn't mean we don't care about things – about our loved ones, our career, our possessions – but it means that we're not attached to them. We are able to appreciate them and let them be.

'When we are in this space we know what has to be done and we know just how to do it. We act in the right way because it is the right thing to be doing at this time and in this place, not because we have any sense of compulsion, any "shoulds" or "should nots". We are in tune, in harmony, part of "now". We know that whatever we do, whatever we say, will be right.'

The monk pauses and Dan catches his eye.

'Yes, do you have a question?' he asks.

'I do some sports coaching', says Dan, 'and I find what you have said about this "inner space" beyond our ego very interesting, because it sounds a lot like what athletes call being "in the zone", or "in the flow". It's a state that just happens when they are totally in their element, exhilarated and sometimes achieving extraordinary performances.'

Dan pauses, then continues quietly, 'I felt it once when I was skiing. The sun was shining, the snow was perfect, I had the speed. It was totally exhilarating, like being part of everything.' He tails off. 'I can't really describe it', he decides, 'but I have read about being "in the zone" and I have seen it described as an almost transcendental experience. That's really what it felt like at the time.'

'I think you *have* described it', says the monk, 'thank you, Dan, and I agree, it is something we can all experience in our meditation – even if we are not skilled athletes! It is what we touch when we're mindful. It is the presence that is always there beneath the chatter of our mind, beneath the voice of our inner critic. It has not arisen; it is just there. Because it has not arisen, it doesn't cease. It is always there: eternal, spacious, free.

'As we empty our mind of everything and touch this place of inner awareness, the feeling of being an individual disappears. Like rays of light within the sun or the tiny ripples within the ocean, we merge. We feel we are one with everyone, yet there's no person there: simply, as Ajahn Sumedho put it, "clarity, awareness, peacefulness and purity."'

The cessation of suffering has been realized

There is complete silence in the room. We are a group of individual people: men and women; all ages from late teens to nearly eighty and seemingly from all walks of life. Yet it feels as though we are all one.

The silence continues for a few more seconds – or minutes – I'm not sure. I've really lost track of time.

Then the monk says, 'When you've touched that place within, when you've experienced a deep peace, joy and luminescence of connectedness with all living beings, with all life; when you've touched that sense of now and eternity all being one, you'll never fear death again.

'You'll be like the wise Buddhist monk who was confronted by a samurai warrior brandishing a sword, taunting, "Don't you know who I am? Don't you know you're in the presence of a man who could run his sword through you without blinking an eye?"

'The monk calmly replied, "And you are in the presence of a man who could let you run your sword through him without batting an eye."

'You see, when you have experienced cessation – and we can all do it in this lifetime if we practise – you free yourself from any fear of death. There is no death because we are already in eternity, in paradise, but most of us just don't realize it.

'But once we *do* realize it, and we touch that paradise within, everything changes. Spirit becomes our reality; lifetimes come and go, but spirit is eternal. We – the real us, that ripple of the ocean of spirit that became clothed in a physical body when we were born – are still part of the ocean. The ripple has simply acquired a physical body for a lifetime – a few seconds of eternity – until it is reunited with the rest of the ocean of spirit – its real self. It has been in paradise all the time, but just hasn't realized this unless it has been blessed enough to find mindfulness meditation and the teaching of another personification of the ocean, known as the Buddha.'

'It's hard to get our head around', says Pam. Then she adds, 'But if in our spirit we are all one – miniscule ripples in a great ocean that we get reabsorbed into when we die – how is it that mediums and people who are psychic can contact those who have passed away? I had an amazing message from my grandad after he had died.'

'In Buddhist teaching there are many realms of existence', replies the monk. 'I think of it like this: the little ripple that is our essence – our essential being, the part of us that never dies, which is also a part of the great ocean within all living beings – is wrapped around by layers, like an onion or a hyacinth bulb.

'The spark of life at the centre is always "in heaven", but when the physical outermost layer dies, there are other, less dense layers. So when we die we can appear in a body of light, like a young and happy version of ourselves made of finer stuff, translucent and lit from within. Anyone who is psychic has seen this.'

'So', Rodney asks, 'is this ocean what the Buddha referred to as *anatta* or 'no-self'? Can you explain to us what that means?'

'Well, I'll try', responds the monk. 'This is one of the biggest questions in Buddhism: whether or not there is a permanent individual spiritual part of us that survives death, a soul, if you like. The Buddha's teaching contains references to past lives, which implies that there is some individual part of us that does not die, but this is not a question that he ever answered directly.

'In the Pali canon, the earliest surviving record of his teaching, it is said that when the Buddha was asked whether or not we have a soul or an individual spiritual "self", he refused to answer the question.

'I need to explain here that the Buddha always said that there are four types of question:
- those that can be answered with a straightforward "yes" or "no";
- those that deserve an analytical answer;
- those that can be answered with another question;
- those that deserve to be set aside.

'This last group of questions – those that deserve to be set aside – are ones for which the answer does not lead to the end of suffering or stress. According to the Buddha, the teacher has to decide which of the four types of question they are dealing with, and answer them accordingly.

'So he would not say either "yes" or "no" to a question that should be set aside, and if you are the person receiving the answer, you have to decide how much the answer has to be interpreted. The Buddha said there are two types of people who misrepresent him: those who draw inferences from statements that shouldn't have inferences drawn, and those who don't draw inferences from those that should.'

Suzi pulls a face and laughs a little. 'Goodness!' she exclaims. I wait for her to add more, but for once she's speechless.

And I must admit I'm feeling a bit confused, too. It's a bit like that famous Donald Rumsfeld speech in which he talked about known knowns (things we know we know) and known unknowns (things we know we don't know), as well as unknown unknowns (things we don't know we don't know). Mind boggling!

But the monk is continuing, 'So the truth is, the Buddha wouldn't deny or affirm the existence of a permanent independent self or soul. Why do you think the Buddha wouldn't answer this question directly?'

The monk pauses and looks around the room, then he says, 'If you consider it in the context of what we have learned in these Noble Truths, the reason for the Buddha's refusal to answer the question is clear on the grounds that it is one of those questions whose answer would not lead to the end of suffering. Can you understand why that is so?'

The monk waits, looking at each of the group in turn. But no one says anything.

'Ask yourself what's behind the question', he says. "Do I have an independent, eternal soul or "self", as the Buddha called it, or not?"'

He explains, 'It's about attachment, and clinging. The very question implies attachment either to having or not to having a permanent soul. We know that attachment to desire is the cause of suffering. Whether the answer to this question is "yes" or "no", it is encouraging attachment to desire – the very thing that we are endeavouring to let go of in order to find inner happiness, freedom and peace.

'So of course the Buddha couldn't, and wouldn't, answer it. For by clinging to the answer, we would not be able to find that awareness and cessation within; we would find ourselves going down a cul-de-sac.'

The monk stops speaking again. I feel a little disappointed, a little depressed. I wanted to believe in an eternal spiritual self.

Then, I see it. Of course, I'm clinging to that idea! Clinging brings pain and suffering and keeps us away from our inner awareness.

But the monk is continuing to speak. 'So, what do we do?' he asks. 'We do what the Buddha has told us to do. We look at the feeling this question brings up inside us – desire, hate, craving, delusion – whatever it is. Then what do we do next? The answer is what we've been doing throughout this course. You must know it by heart now. You could probably even say it with me. We welcome that feeling. We let it be. We let it go. And when we truly let it go, what do we find? Peace, spaciousness, joy, clarity, glorious freedom and a feeling of being at one with all life, with everything. Bliss.'

The monk stops talking. There is a tangible presence in the room. This must be what heaven feels like, I think to myself.

We hold this feeling for a while. Then the monk quietly says, 'I told you the Buddha's teaching is experiential. Some things are beyond the scope of words. But does that help to answer your question?'

There is a quiet murmur of affirmation from the group. Then Rodney comments, 'It's a razor's edge, isn't it? If you ask the wrong question, the question itself prevents you from getting the right answer. It's almost like a riddle.'

'Yes, that is true', replies the monk, smiling. 'You see, in order to find the truth we have to let go of the desire to find it, let go of any preconceived ideas. Trying to put spiritual truth into words we can understand with our mind is like herding cats – impossible!

'That's why in the Zen branch of Buddhism disciples are given koans to meditate on – these are riddles, like the famous question, "what is the sound of one hand clapping?" They help people to get beyond the confines of the mind and find pure spirit.

'A koan can be a useful tool, but the Buddha has actually given us enough clear instructions in the Four Noble Truths. If we follow these, we'll find all the answers. The Buddha assured us of that.'

The monk pauses, then says: 'There's been quite a lot to take in this session. Let us refresh ourselves, give ourselves a little "holiday of the heart" with a standing meditation.'

There is a little sound of surprise from the group. A standing meditation! I never knew you could meditate standing up – and from the atmosphere in the group, I believe I am not the only one. But then, thinking about it, I suppose if you're being mindful, you can do it in any position.

'A standing meditation is a meditation that, surprisingly enough, you do while you are standing up', says the monk with a chuckle.

The group laughs. I think it sounds rather tiring. The monk continues, 'A standing meditation is a very useful practice to have in your bag of tools. It can feel a little strange at first, but when you get used to it you will find it is a wonderful way of both reviving and calming yourself down. It has both qualities, it's the "mint tea" of meditation practices – it both soothes and stimulates, relaxing you when you are tense and refreshing you when you are tired, according to what your body needs at the time.

'Follow me as I take you through it, but only hold the pose for as long as feels comfortable – you may only be able to manage five minutes at first – maybe less. Stop and continue to meditate in your usual sitting position when you feel you have had enough.

'After a while, if you practise regularly – every day if you can – you will find you can hold the pose for 30 minutes – and it is said that if you do that for 100 consecutive days you will certainly be aware of great benefits, both physical and mental, though I must admit I have never done it myself.'

Goodness, I think to myself, how on earth does a normal person have time to do all these things? You'd need to be in a monastery for that. Then I smile to myself because I think I'm sounding like Ed. I wonder how this is going down with him.

'So,' continues the monk, 'if you are ready, let us begin.'

Standing Meditation

'Stand with your feet parallel, shoulder-width apart. Plant them flat on the ground, firmly and securely, so you feel well anchored.

'Bend your knees slightly, so that your sacrum sinks a little but remains straight, and keep your spine straight.

'Round your chest slightly so that your shoulder blades relax around your back and ribs.

'Tuck your chin in slightly and feel your head lifting as if you are being pulled toward the ceiling by a cord.

'Relax your shoulders and let your arms hang down naturally by the sides of your body; feel that there is some space under your armpits.

'Feel the muscles in your face and jaw soften, let your tongue relax.

'I sometimes feel that this posture, with the firmly planted feet, slightly bent knees, straight spine and loose arms, is rather like that of a gorilla. In fact I think of it as "gorilla pose".

'Now look a few metres ahead, with your eyeballs relaxed and a soft gaze. You can keep your eyes open if you wish or you can close them softly.

'Breathe gently, as you normally do in meditation. You might like to focus on your "hara" centre – the area below your navel – and feel that you are breathing into this spot, as this is strengthening and helps the balance.

'Breathe naturally and, as always in mindfulness meditation, whenever you find your thoughts wandering, bring them back to the awareness of your breath and your body.

'When you feel you have had enough, gently open your eyes, sit down and continue your meditation in your normal sitting position.'

I like the feeling of the pose. I feel very firm and secure with my feet planted on the floor – and I do feel a bit like a gorilla, with my arms hanging down loosely by my sides and space under my armpits.

This pose feels both strong and also strangely freeing. I feel supported by my body, but at the same time I do not feel contained by it. It is difficult to describe, but I find I am aware of myself as being apart from my body, which feels as though it is a container for the real me.

I hope that this does not sound too strange. I am surprised how 'spiritual' this rather demanding pose enables me to feel. Perhaps it is the very demands that the pose puts on the body that makes one more aware of the body as being apart from mind and spirit. I don't quite know what is happening, but I can understand why a standing meditation could be so beneficial on many levels.

Having said that, it seems no time at all before I feel I cannot do it any longer, and have to sit down. I look quickly at the group and notice that I am not the first to do this, though many of them are still standing.

I continue to meditate in the usual sitting position. I still feel very 'free' and open in my chest and heart – very clear, as though there is light all around me and I am looking out into space. By some miracle I am not having as many thoughts as I often do when meditating. But as I think this, I realize that that is another thought!

After a while I hear the sound of the monk's gong and, shortly after, I open my eyes. Other people are sitting quietly – no one is still standing. I wonder how much practice it would take to be able to stand for 30 minutes. Goodness, I think, even five minutes would be an achievement. Then I realize I'm back into 'judgment' and 'results' mode.

I close my eyes again for a moment and take another breath. I notice that there is a beautiful atmosphere in the room. No one speaks for a while, then the monk says, 'So how was that? Did you enjoy it?'

Gwyn smiles, then says 'Yes, I did. It is a very different experience, isn't it? Much more demanding than a sitting meditation. Do you do it often in the monastery?'

'I personally do practise standing meditation quite a bit', replies the monk, 'especially during a long session when I feel a little sleepy. I find it is a helpful way of waking myself up.

It is useful, too, because you can often fit in a little standing meditation when you are waiting for something. Just quietly get into it – perhaps without too obviously adopting a "gorilla stance" if you're doing it in a public place', he says with a laugh, 'and take your mindfulness breaths. It is as refreshing as a cup of tea.

'We have done sitting meditation, walking meditation and now standing meditation', says Tim. Do they have different benefits? And are there any other meditation postures that are beneficial?'

I smile to myself. Tim is sounding just like the doctor that he is, almost as if he is taking notes about a medicine he is going to give to a patient.

'They do have different effects on the body, as you will find the more you practise them,' says the monk. 'Sitting is the go-to pose for meditation; if you can only do one, I would recommend that it be this.

'For many people, walking meditation is not as mentally demanding as a sitting meditation, yet it also has great benefits and is practical because it can be fitted in easily – and if you really can't manage to fit in a sitting meditation, see if you can do a 20–30 minute walking meditation.

'As I said before, in the monastery we alternate sitting and walking meditations, and that is a harmonious way of getting the benefits of both – but I don't expect any of you to meditate to that extent', he adds with a smile, 'unless you are on a retreat'.

'So how does standing meditation fit in?' asks Dan. He seems a very practical, down-to-earth guy.

'That is challenging for beginners', says the monk. 'It takes considerable practice before you are able to do it for long periods of time. It is by far the most physically demanding meditation that we do. Generally we save this for times when we need to wake ourselves up – but as I said, it also has a calming effect, so it's also a good one to do if you feel mentally, emotionally or physically hyperactive.

'Try it for yourselves; see how you can fit it into your daily life and notice how it affects you. But continue with your sitting meditation every day and your walking meditation when you can – and remember your mindfulness breaths in between times.

'That sounds a lot when I put it like that', says the monk, 'but you are building on what you have already done. Just keep going, gently. You will feel the benefit if not immediately, then soon. Research has shown this', he says, then adds, laughing, 'along with millions of practitioners over more than two millennia – they can't all be wrong!'

'Quickly returning to your question, though, Dan, we do also do lying meditation sometimes, especially if we are in pain and cannot sit for long periods of time or if we want to be particularly mindful of our bodies.

Then the monk asks, 'So, are we complete?' There are affirmative sounds from the group and smiles. 'Then let us end with our closing chant.'

We chant, we bow, we pick up our things; at the door we bow again toward the shrine and then we go our separate ways.

Quick Review

- When we accept suffering and refrain from commenting on it, blaming ourselves for having it or judging it, that is the start of the healing process, and gradually, little by little, we experience a cessation of suffering.
- We realize that everything in this world that begins, ends. It ceases or dies. So if we become attached to anything or anybody, we know we will suffer when it changes, ceases or dies.
- We can learn to appreciate something fully, to relish it now without clinging: "to care, but not to care".
- When we become mindful and notice our suffering, we look for the attachment to desire that is causing it, then lay aside the desire instead of grasping it. The suffering eventually ceases, leaving peace, freedom and spaciousness.
- As we focus our mindfulness on this inner spaciousness we can perhaps touch that part of us that never changes.
- We don't have to suffer and we don't have to wait until we die for suffering to end. If we put into practice the Third Noble Truth, we can be free and happy right now.

Practice

- Continue to watch your speech – lose those 'shoulds' and 'oughts', and be kind to yourself.
- Remember your mindfulness throughout the day.

- Meditate each day for 20 minutes – preferably a sitting meditation – and a walking meditation if you can do that, too; or just a walking meditation if you can't manage a sitting one. End your meditation with *metta* and say to yourself: 'May I be safe. May I be happy. May I be well and at ease.'
- Try a standing meditation for a minute or two a day and enjoy the refreshment and strength that this brings to you.

Week 5

The Road to Happiness

*I*t's a very warm afternoon and all the windows are open in the shrine room, which is looking particularly beautiful today, as it is decorated with roses from the garden and they are filling the air with fragrance. The monk is here and the course participants are gathering. I'm already sitting in my place, and I'm feeling decidedly sleepy.

There is a reason for this, apart from that after-lunch feeling. I have had a particularly busy week, with three days in London attending photo shoots for the book I am working on.

I do enjoy photo shoots; they are a time when the book really comes alive. Having worked on a book for some time on my own, planning it and developing recipes, I really enjoy being part of a team creating the visuals. Even now, after all these years, I still find it exciting to see shot after beautiful shot being produced. And these days it's exciting to be able to see the shots immediately, thanks to the wonders of digital photography, rather than having to wait for the courier to arrive to take the films to and from the processors.

Food photography now is rather different from how it used to be earlier in my career. In the 1980s, everything was quite heavily styled with accessories, cutlery, napkins and so on, and the food was made to look perfect. It was shot under studio lights – hence the stories about mashed potato being used instead of vanilla ice cream – although I never experienced that kind of fakery.

As the years have passed, fashions in food photography have changed. Now it's all much more relaxed, with food looking 'home made', and photographed in natural light which makes being in the studio all day less demanding. Nevertheless, I do find shoots very tiring, and I have often wondered why. Maybe it's the daily commuting to the studio, the early starts and late nights or all the sitting around while the food stylist prepares the food and the photographer gets set up for the shot. The food stylists I have worked with make an excellent job of it and I love seeing what they do with my recipes.

I'm continuing to muse idly when I hear the sound of the monk's voice bringing me back to the present moment.

'It's good to see you all again', he is saying, looking around the group and smiling.

'Today we reach the halfway point in our course and we can reflect on how much we have done. We have learned to be mindful and to meditate; we are developing a regular meditation practice; and we have considered the first three of the Buddha's Noble Truths.

'That is quite an accomplishment. You now have some useful skills and tools. You have the knowledge, so all you have to do is practise it so that it becomes easy and natural – "practice makes perfect"', he says with a chuckle 'And that's what this second half of the course is all about: putting into practice the teaching, bringing it right into your everyday lives and experiencing all the benefits that this can bring.

'But before we continue with this next stage, would anyone like to ask any questions or make any comments on what we have done so far? Is everything clear to you? How are you getting on with your mindfulness and meditation?'

Tim puts up his hand. 'There is something I have been thinking about, something I would like you to clarify', he says. 'It's about mindfulness.'

He pauses, the monk smiles. 'What is that?' he asks.

'As I understand it', says Tim, sounding thoughtful and serious, 'you said that being mindful means focusing completely on what is happening in the present moment or on one particular activity such as cleaning our teeth, without getting distracted with any thoughts, commenting, judging, comparing, criticizing and so on. Is that correct?'

'Yes', says the monk, 'that is correct.

'In that case', says Tim, 'I am wondering how it is possible to be mindful of the present moment *and* watch the breath? I find I can only focus on one thing at a time.'

The monk pauses for a moment, then replies, 'That is an important point – thank you for raising it, Tim. I will explain.

'Mindfulness, as you know, means paying attention and opening our awareness to what is happening at this moment and accepting it – without commenting, judging, criticizing, comparing or controlling. We just notice or give it "bare attention", as we monks sometimes say. That is being mindful.

'Now we can choose to be open to everything, to get a general sense of all that is happening to us at any moment, or we can narrow down our view and just be mindful of a smaller area.

For example, at this moment we can be mindful of this whole room or we can direct our mindfulness to, say, only our body or to what we are doing at this moment or our breathing. It is like pointing a camera lens at something and then either expanding or contracting the area we are focusing on.

'Once we understand mindfulness, we can focus our "mindfulness lens" on to anything we choose, though the Buddha taught that there are four "foundations" of mindfulness that guide what we point the mindfulness lens at. He said these were:

1   Mindfulness of the body, including the breath.

2   Mindfulness of the emotions and feelings, as we have been learning in the First and Second Noble Truths when we have been noticing "there is suffering", and looking for the cause.

3   Mindfulness of our mind, which is when we endeavour to find that clear space between our thoughts as we meditate.

4   Mindfulness of what the Buddha called "no-self" or "not self", which we spoke of when we considered the Third Noble Truth and asked "who am I".

'So those are the four ways to be mindful and we can choose what we are going to focus on and whether we open our mindfulness lens wide to take in a panoramic view or zoom in close to focus on a blade of grass, a flower or a butterfly's wing.

'Is that clear now?' the monk asks. 'In practice, you don't have to think about whether you're being mindful of your feelings or your thoughts or your body or whatever, you just do it – but I hope this has made the whole process clearer to you.'

I am glad of the monk's explanation. It has certainly clarified mindfulness for me.

Tim seems to be agreeing, but he is asking another question, 'Yes, but I am also wondering about the loving kindness practice you gave us – how is focusing on that being mindful? To me, thinking about *metta* seems to be imposing a thought on top of our mindfulness.'

Tim appears to be making it all sound rather complicated, but the monk seems to follow his meaning.

'*Metta*', replies the monk, 'is more an attitude of mind than a thought, like gratitude, compassion or empathy are. *Metta* is a feeling of love and kindness and an attitude of understanding and of being at one with all sentient beings, united in our suffering and pain, in our longing for love, safety, freedom and peace; and brought together in our sharing of joy, kindness and consideration for one another. When we do our *metta* practice, we focus on someone – ourselves, another person or a particular thing such as the pain in our back, the problem in our mind, the state of the world and so on – and we bring the attitude of *metta* or loving kindness to it.'

The monk pauses for a moment, then he smiles, chuckles a little and says, 'You could think of *metta* as putting a pink filter on the mindfulness lens. When you send out *metta* you are being mindful through a pink lens of loving kindness.'

'Is that clearer now?' asks the monk.

Tim nods.

'So you mean we look at the world through rose-tinted spectacles?' chips in Maurice, smiling.

'Yes', replies the monk, 'you could say that – *metta*-tinted spectacles.'

'Oh, I wish I could buy a pair of those!', says Suzi yearningly and we all laugh.

'Well, maybe you'll get to wear some naturally as you continue your *metta* practice regularly', replies the monk, smiling.

He pauses. Then Debbie, who's looking relaxed, puts up her hand. 'I'd just like to say thank you for suggesting the short meditations', she says. 'I find I can fit in a few mindfulness breaths – what you called mindfulness minutes – in between my clients and at odd moments during the day. I am enjoying it and really noticing the benefit. And when I walk my dog I try to do a walking meditation – as much as he will allow me to', Debbie adds with a laugh. She does seem happier and less tense than she was before.

'I am glad', says the monk, beaming at Debbie. 'Regular mindfulness practice brings calmness and an inner strength that gently permeate your life, so once mindfulness becomes a regular practice, circumstances change – "like attracts like", as they say, and inner calm attracts outer calm.

'As you experience this, I think you will find that your life will allow you the opportunity to meditate for a longer period. You will be able to build up the time gradually, starting with five or 10 minutes and slowly increasing to 20 minutes.

'Research shows that 10 minutes of meditation brings marked results and 20 minutes has an even more pronounced effect on the body and mind.'

The monk pauses, then laughs and says, 'And the most beneficial and pronounced results, physically and mentally, were found in monks who meditated for upward of five hours a day or more – but I'm not asking you to do that!'

We all laugh. I cannot imagine myself ever being able to sit and meditate for such long periods of time – as I've mentioned, 20 minutes seems an age to me at the moment. But Robert has been on one or two Buddhist retreats in which he stayed in a monastery for 10 days and meditated all day, from early in the morning until late at night, alternating sitting meditation with walking meditation, and he found he soon adapted to it. The effects on him were certainly profound.

'You really would have to be in a monastery to do that!' comments Ed.

'Yes', responds the monk, 'and that amount of meditating is not for everyone.'

There is a pause, then Ed adds, 'I can understand the point of meditation and I'm finding it helpful, I have to say. But do you ever think that it is self-indulgent or escapist to go into a monastery?'

I feel really annoyed with Ed. I think the way he seems to like challenging the monk is rude and I wonder whether to say something. But before the words come out of my mouth the monk roars with laughter.

'Escapist?' he says with another laugh, 'No, Ed, I don't think you could say that! We do withdraw from the world, but it is through a sense of vocation – an inner calling, a knowing. We need to be away from the distractions and demands of the world in order to meditate deeply and learn from our contemplation. Becoming a monk and living in a monastery is like entering a period of training in which we study so that we can teach and give something to the world.

'Also, by being in the monastery we help to create a place of peace where people can come for inner sustenance, meditate, find peace and then take it out into their own lives. People come to the monastery from all over the world.'

The monk pauses thoughtfully for a moment, then says, 'The various schools of Buddhism and different monasteries have their own rules. But in the Theravada tradition, although we live in the monastery and abide by strict vows, we follow the Buddha's example of getting out into the world, collecting alms on which we survive and bringing the Buddha's teaching through example – through putting it into practice by being there for people.

'We live in the monastery so that we can abide by the *vinaya* – the Buddha's strict rules for monks. The Buddha gave us these rules to encourage our own spiritual development by being away from the distractions of life that encourage greed, hatred, delusion, clinging and craving and thus enable us to concentrate on our meditation and contemplation.'

'Isn't that cheating – getting away from temptation?' asks Ed, with a laugh.

'No', says the monk. 'It's a case of focus and of choice – how we decide to use our energy. We choose to give up certain things to focus on something that for us is more valuable – spiritual freedom, enlightenment.

'We give up those things so that we can concentrate our energy on our spiritual development rather than constantly having to battle with temptations that have been stirred up by our senses being stimulated by our environment.

'It's just common sense, really, but distancing ourselves from the things that stimulate our senses doesn't mean we don't get plenty of opportunity to practise coping with desire, I can assure you. Human nature is human nature. There's always something you can yearn for or get irritated by.

'But if we want to experience peace and harmony inside ourselves, to free ourselves from the suffering caused by desire (greed, hatred, delusion, clinging and craving), it is helpful not to surround ourselves by things that stir up temptation – without being "attached" to such harmonious conditions, of course. If there happen to be distractions, such as helicopters circling continuously overhead', he says with a laugh, referring to the story he told us earlier, 'then we handle it.

'You know, in life our outer surroundings are a reflection of our inner life and vice versa. Having harmonious outer surroundings helps us to be harmonious within and being peaceful within helps to create peace in our environment.'

The monk stops and Gwyn speaks, 'So you bring healing, understanding and peace to the world, both through your own example and through teaching?' she asks.

'That is a nice way of putting it', replies the monk, smiling. 'We do our best, we do our best.'

After a pause the monk adds thoughtfully, 'I would not be teaching here today if I had not become a monk.

'Being a monk is certainly not for everyone. Of all the people who come to the monastery to train to become monks, only a tiny proportion last the course. Many realize that such a life is not for them and they leave.

'Think of it like this: being a monk is just another way of living and contributing to life, in the same way as being a teacher, a doctor or anything else. Just as a teacher or a doctor has to train in order to do their work, so does a monk. And part of that training consists of following strict rules, which give us the discipline we need for the amount of meditation and contemplation required.'

The monk pauses for a moment then adds, 'You know, we are not allowed to teach until we have been an ordained monk for ten years, or for ten "rains retreats", as we say.

'But I think we are getting a bit off topic here', he continues with a smile, 'although what we have been saying is rather relevant to the Fourth Noble Truth, which we are going to consider today.

'The Fourth Noble Truth is all about putting the Buddha's teaching into practice in our daily lives, supporting our inner work of mindfulness with a way of life that also leads to freedom in the outer world. And that is such a joyous experience... being in the world but not "of the world"; walking in the footsteps of the Buddha; living your life according to the simple but profound principles he laid down; feeling a peace and joy that is beyond words.

'And it is in the Fourth Noble Truth that the Buddha gives us the guidelines for doing exactly this – for *living* the teaching in our daily life.'

The monk's enthusiasm and joy is infectious: there's a feeling of expectancy, almost excitement, in the room.

The Fourth Noble Truth

'The Fourth Noble Truth consists of what the Buddha called The Eightfold Path: eight principles, surprisingly enough', he says with a laugh, 'which, when followed, lead to freedom from suffering.'

When he says this the group stirs. Ed has another question.

'But I thought we had already done that – found a way out of suffering with the first three Noble Truths? That's what you told us before', he says.

'Yes', says the monk, 'that is correct. We have learned to recognize that there is suffering and what causes it – greed, hatred, delusion, clinging and craving. We have also discovered how to free ourselves from suffering– a diagnosis, a remedy and a cure for suffering, if you like.

'But, as any good doctor knows, to make a cure permanent you cannot just send a patient back into the world to live their life in the same old way or they'll be back in the surgery with the same old problems in the blink of an eye. Isn't that so, Dr Tim?' he says with a chuckle.

Tim blushes slightly and laughs. 'Yes, too true, too true', he replies.

'So', the monk explains, 'the Buddha gave us the Fourth Noble Truth, which tells us how to live in a way that supports the inner work we are doing with the first three Noble Truths and leads to freedom and enlightenment. However', he adds thoughtfully, 'the Buddha never made any great claims about anything, he simply said "I teach about suffering: its origin, cessation and path. That's all I teach."'

We're all silent. The monk pauses, then continues, 'So now we've come to what the Buddha referred to as the Eightfold Path, as described in the Fourth Noble Truth. And, like the other three Noble Truths, it has three parts or "insights":

'"There is the Eightfold Path, the way out of suffering.
This path should be developed;
This path has been fully developed."

'The first insight says that we begin with knowing that the Eightfold Path is the way out of suffering; the second insight tells us that we have to follow that path; and the third insight says that we have followed it.

'And I have to say that like the first three Noble Truths' he adds with a laugh, 'it sounds simple but it's a lifetime's work – several lifetimes' work, you might even say.'

The monk smiles, pauses again, then continues, 'In fact, this last Noble Truth – the Eightfold Path – really encapsulates the first three, so once you've understood them, this fourth one is all you need. It says it all and is a formula for happiness that you really can keep in your back pocket.

'So the Eightfold Path consists of eight principles or qualities, which are arranged in three groups that concern wisdom, morality and emotional balance respectively. They're listed like this to help us remember them, but it's important to know that they don't constitute a 'to do' list of things that we tick off one by one. They're qualities that are related to each other, that we develop alongside each other. And as a group they, like the first three Noble Truths, present the way out of suffering and lead to happiness, freedom and peace.

'It seems to get more and more intricate', I say, 'with one thing relating to another; a bit like a set of Russian dolls stacked inside each other.'

The monk laughs. 'Yes', he agrees. 'There is no doubt that the Buddha had a very clever, logical mind. The teaching may seem complicated but it isn't really, and because it's so interrelated, it is very easy to remember once you've got your head around it.

'Another benefit', he says, 'is that it all works together – all clicking into place, each aspect supporting the others – to bring about our development and well-being.'

The monk pauses, then adds with a smile, 'It's like all the parts of the car working to get us to our destination.'

'Or all the dominos falling down when you set the first one off', comments Ed.

The group laughs.

The monk laughs too, then responds, 'Hmm, I'm not sure I like the analogy of everything falling down, but I see what you mean. One thing sets off another and that is exactly what happens – and why practising the Fourth Noble Truth is important because it helps to set the dominoes on their way.'

'But let's get down to business. I have to admit that the way these qualities are named can be a bit off-putting. They are called Right View, Right Intention, Right Speech, Right Action, Right Livelihood, Right Effort, Right Mindfulness and Right Concentration.

'That's a lot of 'Rights', isn't it? They give them rather a judgmental tone, but it's another case of the exact meaning getting lost in translation. The original Pali words mean something closer to "pure", "ideal" or "skilful" ways of living that bring about the happiest, harmonious results, rather than being "right" in the moral sense. For this reason people sometimes refer to them as Skilful View, Skilful Intention and so on, instead.

'But let's not let semantics and prejudice get in the way. We'll stick with the usual translation – "right" – which is good enough and allows the eight principles to speak for themselves. When we are trying to remember the eight principles, it can be helpful to think of them as being symbolized by aspects of a human being.

'The first two, Right View and Right Intention, help us to develop wisdom, and correspond to the head. Then we have three that concern the way we lead our life and describe our behaviour in the world: Right Speech, Right Action and Right Livelihood. These are like the body. And the last three, Right Effort, Right Mindfulness and Right Concentration, are about our motivation – or our heart and feelings, if you like. That's an easy way to remember them.'

I think about this for a moment and wonder how I am ever going to remember them. I try to work out a mnemonic, one of my favourite memory tricks, but I can't invent one, so I stick with the letters at the beginning of each: V, I, S, A, L, E, M and C. That will do for the moment. Sounds like some kind of special type of passport. Maybe it is – sort of.

But the monk is speaking again while my mind wanders. 'We'll study one group at a time', he's saying, 'starting with the "head" group today. And we'll break it down so that we take them one principle at a time. Then we'll consider the other two groups over the next two weeks.'

Sounds like we're going to be busy.

Right View

'The first principle of the Eightfold Path, Right View, really encompasses all the truths expressed in the first three Noble Truths we have already considered. It's a way of looking at things and living your life that leads to freedom from suffering and peace.

'So, Right View, refers to being mindful, being in the present moment, accepting all that this moment contains – "it is as it is". And if this moment contains pain, we learn to stand aside and become the observer, so that we can say, "there is suffering" ("*there is*", remember, not "*I am*").

'And we have seen that when we do this, when we let the suffering be and even welcome it if we can, the suffering decreases and eventually ceases all together. This really does work. Anyone can prove it for themselves.'

The monk pauses, then continues, 'We've also seen how suffering is caused by attachment to desire – "greed, hatred and delusion, clinging and craving" – and how by becoming aware of our attachments and letting them go, we can liberate ourselves from suffering and find inner peace.

'In this process we have discovered the truth that "all that is subject to arising, is subject to ceasing" – in other words, everything that begins, ends. And through being mindful, being fully aware of the present moment, we know that we can touch a constant place of perfect peace, clarity, purity and joy within ourselves.'

The monk pauses. Everyone is silent. For a moment I feel totally at peace, uplifted by his words. It's a slightly warm, glowing feeling, full of strength. His words seem to have brought a 'presence' into the room again. I wonder whether the rest of the group is feeling it, too. I allow myself to relax into the presence and my mind seems to stop for a time – just a few moments, a second or two maybe – I don't know because I've lost track of time. I take a couple of mindfulness breaths. *This is bliss*, I think to myself.

I come back to the sound of the monk's words, 'I know that if you're new to this it's a lot to take in but, I must repeat and emphasize that it's not a difficult or complicated process unavailable to the likes of ordinary people like you and me. Don't let anyone tell you that. Anyone can do it; *anyone*. And the results are so worthwhile – the benefits are priceless, really. So just follow the simple steps we've been given; just do it.'

The monk thinks for a moment, then Rodney catches his eye.

'You make it all sound so simple, but I have been trying to meditate and follow the Buddhist path for several years now and I don't know if I've been making much progress ... ' He tails off, sounding rather disconsolate.

'It *is* simple, but it's not always easy', replies the monk. 'No one can do it *for* you. No one is going to wave a magic wand over you and make it happen. But you have the power within you – we all have – to do it and find happiness, freedom and peace for yourself. That's where the magic comes in.

'So, what I'm saying, Rodney – everyone – is trust your process. Trust the teaching of the Buddha that has been tried and tested down the ages and just do it. The methods work – if you do.

'In the Fourth Noble Truth we have a blueprint for a way of living in the world that supports our inner work and helps us to make progress on the path – not that we think in terms of progress or "results",' he adds with a laugh.

'We need it all: our *inner* work (the meditation, mindfulness, *metta*, and our practice of the first three Noble Truths), alongside our *outer* work, (the way we lead our lives or the Fourth Noble Truth – the 'right' way of living).'

The monk pauses for a moment or two, thinking, then adds, 'You know, that is something some people sometimes forget.'

I wonder what he is talking about, and I don't think I am the only one, because everyone is rather silent. Then Tim pipes up, 'Could you please explain that a little? I am not quite clear what you mean.'

'Yes, of course', replies the monk. 'In the Four Noble Truths the Buddha gave us a complete and balanced formula for living. It's a formula that works, but to get the best results you have to take the whole package – take all the medicine', he says with a laugh.

'It's not as effective if you just take some of it – if you take only mindfulness and meditation, for example, but neglect *metta* and the Noble Truths and just go on living in the same old way. You will certainly get some benefits, because mindfulness and meditation are powerful tools indeed, but when you practise it all – mindfulness, meditation, *metta* and the Four Noble Truths – each aspect supports the others and you get a wonderfully balanced and powerful result.'

'But', the monk says with emphasis, 'we are presented with a bit of a "catch-22" when we try to judge how we are progressing. And why is that?' he asks suddenly.

There is silence in the group, then Rodney answers, 'Because if we are really being mindful, we are concentrating on the present moment, not thinking about how far we have come.'

'Quite so, Rodney, quite so', says the monk; 'and neither are we judging, comparing, or criticizing. We are "being with" things exactly as they are, accepting them. Remember "it is as it is"? I sometimes say, "it is as it is and all is well".

'It sounds so simple, but trust me, it is deep and profound and, if you are looking for "results"', he says, laughing and looking at Rodney, 'that will surely bring them. Try it and see.'

'As our understanding of the Fourth Noble Truth gets clearer and we really make the effort to put it into practice in our lives so that we are *living* the Buddha's teaching in a practical way that truly supports the inner work we are doing, everything comes together; you will see.

'So let us continue. We have looked at the first quality of the Eightfold Path, Right View and now we're moving on to the second quality, Right Intention.'

Right Intention

'"Right intention" – sometimes also known as "Right Thought" – is the other "wisdom" or "head" element. It does mean thinking in the "right" way, but in the original Pali language used by the Buddha it has a more dynamic quality than just thinking in the right way. It's more like having a feeling of hope and optimism within us, making an intention to put into practice the wisdom of the Four Noble Truths in our life, to live them, rather than just think about them

'With Right View we have the knowledge and with Right Intention we have the willpower to use that knowledge – a dynamic combination indeed.

'So, we put in the practice with our mindfulness, constantly bringing ourselves back to the present moment. This in turn means that we accept life as it is, which leads us to trust our intuitive mind and allow the judgment, criticism and comparison of the shallow part of our mind to drop away, so that we are compassionate with ourselves and others. We let go of fixed, conditioned opinions and reactions. We flow with things. We find peace. We use our will, our "right intention", to put into practice the Buddha's teaching.

'When you look at the way life works, doesn't everything begin with a thought, an idea? You think about going on holiday or planning a project – or even writing a book', he says, looking at me.

'They all start with a thought, don't they? How do you create your recipes, Rose?' he asks. 'Don't they all start with a thought, an idea?'

Goodness, that's a surprise. People ask me all the time how I write my recipes, but I wasn't expecting that from a monk in a meditation group! He is right, of course. My recipes always start with an idea – either a picture of a dish in my head or a flavour in my mind; or sometimes the sight of an ingredient I see in a shop or a market. It's often the visual aspect of a dish that really gets my ideas flowing.

I frequently think that I got into cookery writing because I really wanted to go to art school, but my parents and head teacher teamed up to prevent this from happening: my parents because they did not think going to art school was in keeping with the spiritual work they planned for me and my head teacher because she wanted as many pupils as possible to go to university.

In the end, I did neither. As it happened, before I could do any of that, I met Robert, who is considerably older than me, and I was desperate to leave school. When the chef at the retreat centre suddenly left, I took my opportunity and persuaded my parents to let me take over the cooking.

It is a measure of their desperation – vegetarian cooks were few and far between in those days – that they agreed to this, but it was a key moment in my life because the food that I cooked for the guests there was well received and led to me writing my first recipe book and what became my career.

I'm pondering on this and on the power of intention, when Nikki raises her hand and the monk invites her to speak.

'Does "Right Intention" mean what we call "positive thought"? she asks. 'I'm thinking of things like affirmations, visualizing what we want to happen to help it to come about, and so on? I rather like those', she adds.

'That's an interesting question', replies the monk. 'The Buddha said, "all that we are is the result of what we have thought; it is founded on our thoughts, it is made up of our thoughts", so I think that using positive thought might indeed be another interpretation of Right Intention. But there is something we need to be careful of here.'

The monk pauses and looks at Nikki, and around the group.

'Can you see what that is?'

Gwyn, who always looks so elegant in a low-key, casual way, and is wearing a silky cream shirt today, looks up, and the monk smiles at her.

'Yes? he asks, 'do you know the answer?'

'I think we need to remember the Second Noble Truth. It would be easy to get attached to what we want to bring about or to have – wanting, not wanting and all the rest of it', she says.

'Exactly', says the monk, 'we need to watch out for our old friends greed, hatred, delusion, clinging and craving. We need to be careful that in aspiring or intending, we don't get dissatisfied with the present, caught up in desire and attached to outcomes – *attached* to what we want for the future.'

'So', persists Nikki, 'does that mean that it's OK to use positive thought, affirmations, and visualizations to create better conditions in our lives? I find that helpful, but now I'm wondering whether it goes against the Buddha's teachings.'

'No', says the monk, 'as I'm saying, intention is a very important part of the Buddha's teaching. "Action follows intention", he said. In fact, if I may say so, if you look at "New Age" writing about positive thought, affirmations, the law of attraction and so on, you'll see they all go directly back to the Buddha, 2,500 years ago.'

'I didn't know that', I say. 'Why don't they acknowledge the source then?'

'Maybe they don't realize', replies the monk, with a shrug. 'Or maybe they think of Buddhism as a religion and don't like the idea of using techniques and methods that are part of a so-called religious practice. But as I mentioned at the beginning of this course, the Buddha never claimed his teaching was a religion.'

'Maybe they don't realize that, either', laughs Tim.

The monk stops to gather his thoughts, then says, 'All the Buddha did, as he himself said, was offer his teaching freely for everyone to use to alleviate suffering. That became his life-purpose, simply that. "I teach about suffering and the way out of suffering, that is all I teach", he said.'

The monk pauses again, then adds thoughtfully, 'But the Buddha's teaching is a lot more profound than that, as we are discovering for ourselves. I think he would be joyful to see how widely his teaching is used today and how many millions of people throughout the world are helped by it, even if the source is not acknowledged. After all, he had worked hard to dismantle the building that was his ego, if you remember, so I don't think he needs us to start building it up again.'

I am feeling a bit irritated on behalf of the Buddha that his teaching has been so widely adopted without attribution. Then I realize that my annoyance is making me unhappy and I am spoiling my own inner peace as a result. I smile to myself, take a deep breath and let the irritation go.

'But to return to your original question, Nikki', the monk continues, 'it all depends how you use your positive thought, affirmations and so on. I would say it's perfectly fine to visualize conditions or a future that you wish to create for yourself: beautiful conditions, peace and happiness; even physical things that you would like to have in your life. But you have to do so without clinging, craving, becoming attached to the outcome or becoming deluded.'

The monk laughs a little. 'Can you do that, do you think? Visualize, even pray, then let it go?'

When the monk says this, I remember something I read years ago in a book on visualization. It said to picture what you 'want' – if I can use that word – then 'see' it inside a pink balloon and let it go into the sky, trusting that it will happen if it's the right thing for the highest good.

'You can visualize and intend conditions', continues the monk, 'and imagine how you would feel if you had them. You can even get to the point where you can feel now the joy and happiness you would feel if they were already part of your life, as long as you don't become attached to them or unrealistic about the practicalities of life.

'It's a bit of a balancing act, but you can give the seeds the right conditions to sprout and grow by finding peace and contentment in the present moment in the ways we have discussed in the first three Noble Truths and through feeling gratitude for everything.

'So', continues the monk, looking at Nikki, 'can you visualize or affirm something without becoming attached to the outcome and while feeling gratitude for what you already have?'

Nikki pulls a face, and laughs a little. 'I'm working on it', she replies.

'As you get more and more into the teaching, you will find that you rely less and less on external conditions for your happiness and peace of mind', the monk adds. 'You may even get to the point when you have so much peace and joy within you that you are truly happy and contented in this moment, whatever is going on around you – you might even call that "heaven on Earth", or "*nirvana* now"' he adds, with a chuckle.

There is a silence, then the monk carries on, 'Perhaps it would be helpful to know that the Buddha did give additional guidance on what he meant by "Right Intention". He said there are three kinds of "Right Intention", or "right" ways of positive thinking. The first is the intention to let go of our attachments – anything we cling to, depend upon for our happiness – because, as we know from the first three Noble Truths, clinging can only lead to suffering; in the long run, it does not bring us peace and happiness.

'And we have already been working on the second "right" intention that the Buddha gave, and that is good will or *metta*. We make the intention to bring loving kindness first to ourselves and then for *metta* to spread to all those around us, all who come into contact with us, then to the whole world, eventually. And when we really do that, we feel so much joy and contentment that we naturally begin to let go of our desires.'

The monk stops for a moment, then continues, 'And that leads on to the Buddha's third "right" intention, which is "harmlessness", or not doing harm, not hurting, not being violent to anything but being compassionate to all living beings. That really follows on from *metta*, because when you truly feel loving kindness in your heart, you cannot hurt or harm another living being.'

We are all silent, then Robert says quietly, 'That's a lot to ask.'

'Yes', replies the monk, 'but it is the path to happiness, as many have found before us and many will find after us.'

The monk thinks for a minute, then smiles and says, 'You know, the Dalai Lama expressed the essence of what we are saying very simply and powerfully when he said, "Love and compassion are necessities, not luxuries. Without them humanity cannot survive". And the thing is, when we give out love and compassion to others, we benefit ourselves. And *vice versa*. When we are loving and kind to ourselves we are able to be kinder to others, as we have been discovering in our *metta* practice'.

'It all fits together, as we were saying earlier and, yes, it does get easier. Just make a start. Begin in little ways, as we have been doing over the last few weeks with mindfulness breathing, a daily meditation, *metta* practice, being kind to yourself – building up your pool of peace and loving kindness within. You will be surprised how effective all of that is.'

We are all rather quiet. There is a thoughtful mood in the group. Then the monk continues, 'So those are the first group of principles of the Eightfold Path: Right View and Right Intention. Next time we will consider the second group of principles.'

The monk pauses, then says, 'But now, let us cherish ourselves with a body-scan meditation to close this session. Have any of you done a body-scan meditation before?'

There are a few sounds of affirmation from the group, though most of us are silent. The monk explains, 'The body-scan meditation originated in Burma, or Myanmar as it is known today. It is quite widely used in Theravada monasteries and is a useful practice to know. It is a little like the relaxation that some of you may have done, perhaps at a yoga session,' he continues, 'but it is not to be confused with relaxation – it is different.'

'Why is that?' asks Nikki. 'How they are different?'

'In one simple way,' explains the monk. 'In a relaxation there is a goal: to relax. In a body-scan meditation, as in any Buddhist meditation, there is no goal. You are simply being mindful of your body, opening yourself to your body at this very moment, exactly as it is, pain and all, accepting, letting be, letting go'.

'When you do this at home, you can do it lying down,' he continues. 'Place a small cushion or a folded blanket under your head, and position your legs so that your feet are planted on the floor where your knees would be if you were lying straight out, with your hands loosely by your side.

'You can do that today if you like – and can find enough space – but it is also perfectly acceptable to do a body-scan in a normal seated meditation position.'

We move quietly into position, with most of the group sitting and some lying on the floor as the monk described. He waits quietly until we have all stopped moving.

'If you are ready, we shall begin.'

Body-Scan Meditation

'Often we begin a mindfulness meditation by opening our awareness to our body, just as we have done before. This brings us right into the present moment and is always helpful. But in a body-scan meditation, awareness of our body is our main focus.

'So become aware of the firm floor beneath you, supporting you. Allow yourself to relax, to melt into it.

'Bring your awareness to your breath. Take several mindfulness breaths, noticing the air entering your nostrils, flowing into your lungs, then out through your nostrils.

'Feel your breathing become slower. If you become aware of any aches and pains, breathe into them, accept them. Allow them to be as they are.

'We are going to scan our body in horizontal strips, starting with our feet and working up. Keep your awareness of your breath by breathing into the different parts of your body as we come to them.

'So open your awareness to your left toes, be mindful of them; then move your attention to the sole of your left foot. Feel the firmness of the floor beneath it. Keep breathing steadily ...

'Next, move your attention to your left ankle and slowly up your left shin, knee, thigh, all the way up to your hip. Keep breathing into the parts of the body as we reach them.

'Now shift your awareness to your right toes, the sole of your right foot and slowly up to your right ankle, shin, knee, thigh to your hip. Breathe steadily ...

'Very slowly continue up your body to your lower back and abdomen, your upper back and chest; then your shoulders. Breathe steadily …

'Now move your awareness over to your left fingers, hand, wrist, lower arm, upper arm and shoulder. Breathe steadily …

'Next, focus on your right fingers, hand, wrist, lower arm, upper arm and shoulder. Continue to breathe steadily …

'Bring your awareness to your neck, your throat, then your jaw – allow it to relax. Now focus on your eyes – allow them to soften and relax. Shift your attention to your forehead, the back of your head, the top of your head. Breathe steadily …

'Give yourself to the breath. Breathe in, breathe out. Let it go in … out.

'Feel the peace. It is as it is. All is well.

'When you are ready, gently open your eyes. Take a few more breaths and then slowly move when it feels right.

I love this meditation. I find it easier to keep my mind free from stray thoughts as I go up the body. I do not know how long we have been meditating, but is seems no time at all before the monk sounds the gong.

We move; we open our eyes. I look around. There is a beautiful feeling in the room.

The monk smiles. 'Are there any questions?' he asks.

I feel so relaxed and peaceful that I cannot think of a thing to say. In fact, I don't really want the peace to be disturbed, but Tim has something to ask.

'Is that meditation we have just done something that could be used to bring pain relief?' he wonders.

'Yes', says the monk, 'it can. And it is used for that purpose. You can do a mini body-scan meditation any time you feel pain or tension in your body. Open your awareness to the pain, allow it to be. Be one with it and enfold it with *metta*.

'And that brings us almost back to where we started this session,' says the monk with a smile. 'Next time, we will go more deeply into how a body-scan meditation can be used to help with pain. But for today, if you are complete, let us join together in our closing chant.

We chant, then we bow and leave quietly.

Quick Review

- The Fourth Noble Truth consists of the 'Eightfold Path' – a set of eight guidelines for living in a way that supports the inner work we are doing and leads to happiness, freedom and peace.
- The first two principles are Right View and Right Intention.
- Right View means being mindful, being in the present moment, accepting all that this moment contains. If it contains pain, we learn to observe it – "there is suffering" – and welcome it, so that the suffering decreases and eventually ceases.
- Right Intention means resolving to continue with our mindfulness practice, accepting life as it is and allowing judgment, criticism and comparison to drop away.
- The Buddha said there are three kinds of Right Intention:
  - letting go of our attachments – anything we cling to or depend upon for our happiness – because, as we know from the first three Noble Truths, clinging can only lead to suffering; in the long run it does not bring us happiness, freedom and peace.
  - bringing loving kindness or *metta* first to ourselves and then to all those around us so that we are compassionate to all living beings.
  - practising harmlessness, or not doing harm, hurting or being violent toward anything.

Practice

- Think of ways you are practising Right View and Right Intention in your life, and how you can extend or strengthen these.
- Continue with your mindfulness practice.
- Meditate each day for 20 minutes; try a body-scan meditation.
- Continue with your *metta* practice at the end of your meditation, starting with yourself as usual, then add someone who has been kind and supportive to you. The Buddha described them as 'a patron': perhaps a parent, a teacher or a helpful boss. So say to yourself: 'May I be safe. May I be happy. May I be well and at ease.' Then picture your patron and say, 'May you be well. May you be happy. May you be safe and at ease'.

Week 6

Living Mindfully

I am sitting in the shrine room, along with most of the group participants, waiting for the last one or two people to arrive. The monk, too, is here, sitting serene and upright, emanating peace.

People are gathering, quietly slipping into their places, looking happy and relaxed. There is an atmosphere of warmth and friendship, and of anticipation.

I am feeling pleased to see everyone again, to be back in this quiet meditation space, to be participating in this course. I can't help contrasting how I am feeling now with how I was feeling just a few weeks ago when the group began: I was tense, nervous, a bit defensive; almost gritting my teeth.

It is strange because initially I joined in for love of Robert and yet I have got so much back for myself. I am so much calmer, freer, at ease with myself; just, well, *happier*. Sorry, I can't stop using the 'h' word.

I smile to myself thinking that maybe this is an example of good karma that people talk about: you do something kind and you get something lovely back in return. I remember reading in some New Age book that karma comes back multiplied by ten. But who knows? Who's counting, anyway? And if you do something kind in order to receive good karma, does that count?

Not that I held the course here in order to get good karma – the thought never entered my head. Whatever motive provokes it though, it seems from the monk's teaching that you can't have too much *metta*, too much loving kindness in life. Maybe there are times when you have to go through the motions to get into the habit of doing kind things and get that 'kindness muscle' working.

I'm still idly musing when the monk lights the candles, then the incense stick. I watch as the scented smoke spirals upward. I am feeling more comfortable about the simple rituals we perform. I have always loved the smell and the smoke of incense, but I am surprised to say that now I rather enjoy the sound of the words in the short chant we do, even though I don't fully understand them because they are in Pali.

It must be something they put in the incense sticks, some kind of 'happy drug', I think smiling to myself. Then, *I must pull myself together, what is the matter with me.* Luckily the sound of the monk's voice brings me back down to earth, back to my senses, back to the present moment.

'Welcome', he is saying. 'How have you been? How are you getting on with your first part of the journey on the Eightfold Path? Does anyone have any questions?'

There is silence. I wonder whether the rest of the group is experiencing the same slightly sleepy-Sunday-afternoon feeling as I am.

'Let's get straight on then, shall we?' says the monk after a little pause. 'You can ask me any questions as they arise.

'So, just to recap, last time we considered the Buddha's Fourth Noble Truth called the Eightfold Path, which is his road map for our journey through life. It is his guidance for living in the world in a way that supports our inner work – our mindfulness, *metta* and meditation – just as they, in turn, support and strengthen us in our day-to-day living.

'The whole point of the Buddha's teaching, as you know', he adds, 'is giving us a way out of suffering, so that we can find happiness right now. Remember what got the Buddha started on his mission?'

The monk pauses for a moment and looks around the room, then, before we have time to collect ourselves and think of the answer, he continues, 'It was the shock of seeing suffering, wasn't it? Protected and isolated from it as he was, he escaped from the palace into the town and saw the kind of lives that ordinary people lived: the pain, the sickness and the death.

'"I teach about suffering and the way out of suffering; that's all I teach", he said – remember? And that teaching was – is – very simple, but very thorough. It involves inner work – our mindfulness, *metta,* and meditation – *and* outer work – the way we lead our lives in the world. It's a complete package or recipe, if you like', he says, looking at me, 'or maybe you could call it a "prescription"', he adds looking at Tim, the doctor.

The group laughs, I blush a bit. Although I am perfectly happy to stand up in front of 300 or more people doing a cookery demonstration or in front of the camera being filmed, I am actually rather shy and don't much like being singled out.

So that's something for me to work on, I think to myself. *Why don't I like that – being singled out?* I think for a minute and discover that it's fear that lies behind it; fear of disappointing people. And I realize exactly where that came from.

As I've said before, my grandmother was a spiritualist medium – a very good and celebrated one in her time, giving evidential messages to people who had lost loved ones in the two World Wars. My father did not lose anyone close to him in the war, but I'll never forget something he told me that my grandmother said to him after his dad, who was a farmer in the Yorkshire Dales, died.

'I'm getting your father', she said, 'he's got a sheep dog with him. He's showing me a watch and he's saying he's pleased that you've got his watch.'

My dad replied that, yes, he had inherited his father's beloved watch and it meant a lot to him. There was a pause, then my grandmother continued 'But he's saying that he's got "the other watch" with him in spirit, and you will know what he means. When he got to the spirit world, the other watch was there waiting for him. I'm sorry, I don't understand what he means.'

My father did. Tears began to stream down his face. '"Watch" was the name of my dog that died when I was a boy – the dog I really loved', he said, laughing and crying at the same time. That was the sheep dog you were seeing with my father.'

I still get a lump in my throat when I think of this story.

But I've got side-tracked. As I've mentioned before, my grandmother's gift of mediumship led her to start the religious organization and retreat centre where I grew up, and where people came to learn about spiritual matters and to meditate. She was supported in her work by her two daughters, my mother and my aunt and their husbands, my dad and my uncle. We all lived at the retreat centre, which was visited by many rich and eminent people of the time, including members of the aristocracy, eminent writers and high-ranking officers in the forces.

My grandmother envisaged her work continuing long after her time, carried on by her family. Although she was a humble woman in many ways, she was treated with the greatest respect by the visitors who came from all over the world. 'The family', as we were called, was treated similarly and expected to play our part.

We had to prepare for our 'future work', so it was elocution lessons every Saturday morning to enable us to speak well in public (when I would much rather have been learning to ride a horse) and we were expected to be on good behaviour at all times. One of my mother's favourite sayings was 'from those to whom much is given, much is expected'. Not that we ever had much money, but we were greatly loved. I thrived in the beautiful surroundings and the spiritual atmosphere.

So we had a lot to live up to. And from an early age – for as long as I can remember – my sister and I had to put on our best frocks and go and 'meet and greet' all the members of each retreat. There are black and white photos of us, some when we were as little as about five or six and seven or eight years old respectively, with members of these groups in posed, 1950s photos.

As you can imagine, we did not enjoy these visits – being looked at, spoken to and sometimes hugged by people we did not know, people who thought our grandmother was some kind of saint. And that, I realized in a sudden flash, was why I have to this day a fear that people will be disappointed in me when they meet me. In my heart, as a tiny girl, I knew I could not live up to people's expectations. Julia Roberts sums up my feelings beautifully in one of my favourite films, *Notting Hill*, in which she plays a famous celebrity who says words to the effect of, "I'm just an ordinary girl … who wants to be loved …" Ooh, cue the violins.

The funny thing is that although I left that life behind when I moved away from the retreat centre, in the life that I created for myself after that as a cookery writer, I unconsciously set up something rather similar with the public appearances, book signings and cookery demonstrations that became a part of it.

Whenever I make public appearances I am always afraid I will disappoint people and for many years when I was younger I used to worry that they would be disappointed when they tasted my food, because I had been called 'the queen of vegetarian cooking' and people built up high expectations.

It always made me think of something that Marilyn Monroe said, admittedly about a rather different scenario, 'Men expect so much and I can't live up to it. They expect bells to ring and whistles to whistle, but my anatomy's the same as any other woman's. I can't live up to it.' I feel the same about people and their expectations of my cooking.

Suddenly the monk's voice interrupts my reverie. 'So,' he is saying, 'the Buddha's "recipe for living" or "prescription for happiness" consists of three Noble Truths that enable us to understand our suffering and how to free ourselves from it, plus the fourth, in which we back that up with a way of life that supports our mindfulness and inner work – a path to happiness, if you like.

'Just to refresh your memory, this path has eight principles that are put into three groups, corresponding to qualities relating to the mind, the body and the emotions. We looked at the mental ones last time: Right View, and Right Intention, so now we come to the second group, the 'action' principles that correspond to our body.

'In this group we have Right Speech, Right Action and Right Livelihood. It is sometimes described as "morality" or "ethical conduct" – *sila* is the Pali word. As we become more mindful, we begin to realize that the way we behave toward other people has a direct result on how they behave toward us.'

The monk pauses and Nikki raises her hand. The monk smiles, acknowledging her and inviting her to speak.

'Do you mean *karma*?' she asks, pushing back her long, shiny, brown hair. 'We get good karma if we're kind, bad karma if we're not? People often talk about karma.'

'I know they do', replies the monk, laughing a little. 'The word "karma" has become rather misunderstood and misused. There's nothing woo-woo or weird about it.

Karma simply means "action" and if you take certain actions, you'll get certain results: put your hand in the fire, you'll get a burn; bump your head, you'll get a bruise. Do a kind deed, you'll feel happy and peaceful – and you might get a good deed back, but don't do it for that reason', he says, chuckling again.

He continues, 'It is sometimes expressed as "what goes around, comes around", though I'm not very fond of that description because it encourages a lot of speculation: people making judgments about what happens in their lives or in the lives of others as being their "karma", or the result of "bad things" they are supposed to have done or thought in the past. Now that kind of speculation is getting right away from the Buddha's truth, isn't it?'

He pauses, looks around the group and asks again, 'So why is that interpretation of karma – relating it to the past – out of keeping with the teaching of the Buddha?'

No one answers.

'I will tell you', the monk says. 'What is the constant message of the Buddha? Be in the present. Bring your mind back to what you are experiencing *now*. When your mind starts to wander and embroider a situation: *I shouldn't have done this; it was his fault, so it must be my bad karma because I was nasty to him in ancient Rome.* Simply bring it back to the present!'

The group laughs, but the monk continues, 'Careless and ill-informed talk about karma causes pain and confusion. Please note that. I will repeat it: *careless and ill-informed talk about karma causes pain and confusion.*

'It comes under the category of "delusion" (one of the causes of suffering, remember) and just leads you down a cul-de-sac. Don't do it. If you want to find inner peace and joy, don't go back to what you imagine you might or might not have done in ancient Rome or any other place!'

The monk pauses for a moment, and then says: 'I once had a conversation with a man with anger issues who was trying to find peace, but he said he couldn't help his fiery temper because he had been a samurai warrior in a past life.'

We all laugh.

'Many people struggle with anger', explains the monk, 'but that's an excuse I'd not heard before.'

'But what about past-life regression and karma?' asks Nikki. 'I have read that this can bring healing to people.'

'That may be true', responds the monk. But in all my years of experience in my own life, in my teaching and in the monastery, I have found you simply do not need to go digging away to see what past life your current problem might, or might not, be linked to. How does that help? It is just imbuing the pain with other factors, other layers, other scenarios. No, no. The past is over.

'Bring your mind to the present; watch your breath. Follow the Buddha's simple teaching of mindfulness; acknowledge the pain: "there is suffering". If you're looking for the cause, trace it back to what's causing it *now* in the form of greed, hate, delusion, clinging or craving, or a mixture of these things. And most of all, accept – even welcome and embrace – the pain and then let it be.

Become aware of that inner freedom, spaciousness and clarity deep within you, *now*.'

The monk sounds stricter and more serious than I've heard him before. I wonder why. Then he says: 'You see, in my time of teaching as a monk, I have never met anyone who has been helped and healed by the knowledge that they did or did not go through any experience as part of their past karma. But I have met those who have been confused and upset by being told by someone that their current conditions have come about as a result of bad things they have done in a past life.'

The monk stops for a moment, then adds, 'I have also known others who have felt that the fact that they think someone did something to them in a past life gives them the license to do it back to them in their current life – delusion building on delusion.

'So, you see why I said before that "careless and ill-informed talk" about karma causes pain and confusion. Stick to the Buddha's basic teaching. Keep it pure and simple; that's the way forward.

'But to come back to your original question, the Eightfold Path *is* connected with karma, but in the Buddhist sense of "action". And what this means is that the eight principles describe ways to think, act and behave as well as ways to make sure that your actions do not bring consequences that cause you, or anyone else for that matter, suffering. And remember, you do not need to look beyond this lifetime for the consequences.

'When you follow the principles in the Eightfold Path you will feel in harmony within yourself; you will open your heart, you will feel compassion. This may well attract harmony and love into your life, because that's what happens. Kind actions tend to lead to kind responses.

'Now, I have to tell you that the Buddha did take this a stage further and say that by following the Eightfold Path we do not create bad karma for the future, so we avoid entanglements that perpetuate suffering. He said, "According to the seed that is sown, so is the fruit that you reap. The doer of goodwill gathers good results. The doer of evil reaps evil results; if you plant a good seed, then you will enjoy the good fruits."

'But here we're talking about possible karma in the future, we're not delving around to try and find karmic reasons from the past for our suffering now; and I do not believe in making any predictions about creating karma for some "future life", either.'

The monk pauses, then says, 'If you study life, you find we do not usually have to look very far into the future to see the results of our actions. But having said that, part of the Buddha's teaching is definitely about keeping ourselves clean and pure karmically, so that we are not chained to this physical life by repercussions from past actions that need sorting out. So we're not, as the Buddha put it, "stuck on the cycle of re-birth" in order to clean up karma that we have made.

'Karma is our own affair; it's not for anyone to judge another's karmic situation. Thinking like that can easily draw you once again into dreams and delusions. So my advice is to keep in the present, put into practice the Four Noble Truths including the

Eightfold Path and experience the happiness and peace that this brings into your life here and now. And it will; that I promise you.'

'But does what you have been saying mean that we have to believe in reincarnation, then, to make sense of Buddhism? asks Maurice.

'You do not *have* to believe in anything', replies the monk. 'The Buddha was very clear about this, "Believe nothing, no matter where you read it or who said it, no matter if I have said it, unless it agrees with your own reason and your own common sense", he said.

'Oh, I *love* that man!' enthuses Pam. 'How liberating. What an amazing person the Buddha was! I think I'm falling in love with him.'

'Me, too', agrees Suzi.

I smile to myself; I couldn't agree more.

'Oh, I find that so freeing', says Maggie, 'I was brought up in a strictly religious family. I used to have nightmares about burning in hell.'

'Sounds as though the Buddha has quite a fan club', laughs the monk, "Team Buddha", eh? But you see, as I've said, the teaching of the Buddha is experiential. It's all about finding our own way to inner peace and joy. As he himself would say, he just points the way.'

'But what do you think about reincarnation?' persists Pam.

'I think we're getting a bit off the point, here', the monk replies. 'We'll still be here at midnight, if we go on like this. You see how thinking and talking about karma and reincarnation can take us away from the present moment?'

The monk smiles and chuckles, then adds, 'We may talk a bit more about this in another session if there is time. But now, let's come back to the present. Let's consider Right Speech.'

Right Speech

'Speech is powerful, isn't it? I think we are becoming more and more aware of this in these days of easy, instant, world-wide communication. Taking guidance from this principle, Right Speech, and really making an effort to put it into practice could have far-reaching effects in our lives and in the world.

'Everybody says they want to see a more peaceful world and watching our own speech is a powerful way in which each and every one of us can help to bring this about. That's an empowering thought, is it not?

'So what exactly is Right Speech? The Buddha gave clear guidance on this. He said we are *not* using Right Speech if we're: lying or exaggerating – making something sound more dramatic than it really is; speaking with a "forked tongue" – saying one thing to a person's face and something else behind their back; or using filthy language and insulting or abusing people.

'But to put it in a positive way, in the words of Buddha to his monks, we are using Right Speech if: "It is spoken at the right time; it is spoken in truth; it is spoken affectionately; it is spoken beneficially; or it is spoken with a mind of goodwill.'"

This takes me back in my mind to something my mother used to say to me years ago when I was a little girl. I suddenly hear her voice in my head.

The monk looks at me. 'Do you have something you'd like to say, Rose?' he asks.

I feel slightly embarrassed: is this man telepathic? 'No', I reply, 'what you said just reminded me of something my mother used to say to me when I was a little girl, that's all.'

'Is it something you'd like to share?' he asks.

Not really; but the group is listening. I blush. All eyes are on me. I feel I have to speak.

'Only that my mother often told me that before I spoke I needed to ask myself: "Is it wise? Is it true? Is it helpful? Is it kind?" and only to say what I intended if it ticked all these boxes.'

'Your mother clearly was a wise woman', responded the monk. 'It's helpful to guide children in that way – and to show them by example. We can each become an example of the Buddha's teaching. We do not need to say much – in fact, we do not need to say anything at all to be a powerful source of good in the world, a light shining in the darkness. It's true that deeds speak louder than words, but when we do use words, let's remember their power. The Buddha said, "The tongue is sharp like a knife; it kills without drawing blood."'

The monk pauses, then continues, 'Think about it. "The tongue is sharp like a knife; it kills without drawing blood", he repeats.

That's something worth remembering before speaking or sending off a quick text or email.'

There is silence, then Tim remarks, 'I find this one difficult. I think I'm naturally quite critical. I often make cutting remarks.'

'Me, too', agrees Suzi. 'I would find it hard not to gossip with my girlfriends.'

'Yes', agrees the monk. 'Right Speech sounds such a simple principle to put into practice, yet when it comes to it, it's one that many people find really challenging.'

'So what can we do?' asks Pam. 'Surely how someone takes our words is their responsibility. They don't *have* to react, they don't *have* to become insulted or hurt – that's what we've been learning with the first three Noble Truths, isn't it?'

'Quite so', agrees the monk. 'We each have to take responsibility for our actions, but that includes what we say, as well as how we react to another's words.

'We can stop a chain of negativity by not retaliating when someone says – or for that matter, does – something hurtful; we can simply let it go. But, of course, it is better if it's not said in the first place.

The monk thinks, then says, 'Do you remember the story I told you before, about how the Buddha responded to the angry young man who was shouting at him at a public meeting? The Buddha remained completely calm and told him that his anger, like a present he might be giving, still belonged to him if the person he was directing it to refused to accept it.

'That applies not only when someone is angry with you, but also when they are apparently insulting you or putting you down. If you don't accept the insults and "put downs", if you don't let them get to you, then they still belong to the person who is "giving" them to you.

'Another very helpful piece of advice I had when I was training to be a monk was to get into the habit of pausing for a moment or two before speaking. Pause and notice your breath. You will find that doing this naturally brings you back to your centre – and the more you have been practising your mindfulness, the easier and more natural you will find it.

'Get into the habit of asking yourself what is behind the remark you want to make. Is it because something has hurt you? Or stirred up an unpleasant memory? Is it because you want to "get back" at someone? Or do you think that what you're going to say will make you seem clever, successful or important – and if so, why do you need to feel that? Why do you need to add another brick to the building inside you that is your ego?'

We're all quiet. I wonder whether everyone is thinking, as I am, of the many ways we fall short of putting Right Speech into practice.

'Look', the monk says kindly after a while, 'being aware of the power of speech and making the intention to follow Right Speech is a huge first step. Just do it; just do it. As with everything else, including all the truths we have been discussing today, when you just do it, it gets easier. Make that intention, take that plunge.

'After a very short time, it becomes a habit. Then you will find the urge toward Right Speech becomes so strong that you cannot think or say anything critical or unkind because it feels so uncomfortable to you – then you'll really know you're getting to grips with Right Speech.'

'Or you could pinch yourself', says Suzi, 'or wear an elastic band around your wrist and flick it when you say or think something mean.'

'There are lots of things you can do', replies the monk, smiling. I have known people who have a small pebble in their pocket, and they squeeze it when a negative thought arises. But don't be too hard on yourselves. Making the intention to do it is ninety-nine per cent of the task, and gentle persistence accounts for the rest. 'Remember the Chinese saying: "A thousand-mile walk begins with the first step". And the Buddha said something similar, "A jug fills drop by drop". Step by step, drop by drop. Simply intend, notice, be aware and soon, looking back, you'll see how high the jug is filling up.'

We are all quiet, thoughtful. Outside the windows the garden is bathed in sunshine – a perfect summer's afternoon.

The monk looks around the group and smiles.

'So, says the monk, 'after Right Speech, what is next?' 'Right Action', he replies, answering his own question.

Right Action

'What is Right Action? In short, it is behaving in a way that will not bring harm to ourselves or others. This is how the Buddha put it: "Abstaining from taking life; abstaining from stealing; abstaining from unchastity. This, monks, is Right Action."

'The Buddha did elaborate on this for the sake of lay followers, embodying these principles in what we call the Five Precepts, the list of ways of behaving correctly as described by the Buddha:

- Not killing
- Not stealing
- Not misusing sex
- Not lying
- Not abusing intoxicants

We are all silent, then Tim speaks, 'Those all sound clear and reasonable. But how far should we take these things? I can understand about not taking life – but does that mean that it's wrong in every case? I'm thinking about the big issues of euthanasia and abortion – and also isn't it more merciful to put my dog down if he is in pain at the end of his life, rather than to let him continue to suffer? And does the 'no killing' rule mean that all Buddhists are vegetarian? How far do you take this 'no stealing' thing? Do you actually have to be *given* something? What if you find something that someone has obviously discarded – is it OK to pick that up?'

'That's a lot of questions!' responds the monk. 'First of all, it's helpful to remember that these principles of Right Action were given by the Buddha as guidelines. The Buddha points the way; the language he uses is not absolute.

'He says to "abstain from"; he gives guidance as to the Right Action to take to lead a life free from suffering – whether it's our own suffering or the suffering of others, now and in the future.

'The Buddha gave certain basic principles that can help if we bear them in mind.

'While he did not condone the taking of life – any life, incidentally, the life of any living being – he also advocated, above all else, loving kindness, compassion and understanding, as well as being non-judgmental and respecting the right of every human being to make their own decisions.

'And when considering the implementation of these Five Precepts of good behaviour, we have to remember, too, the Second Noble Truth', says the monk, and pauses.

We are all silent. Some of the group, no doubt, like me, are trying to recollect exactly what the Second Noble Truth says.

'Because', continues the monk, 'it's very easy to become "attached" to rules and regulations. And where does "attachment" lead? To suffering', he adds, answering his own question.

'You see, the "absolute" position, which happens when we become too attached to dogma, fails to take into account our human nature completely. Doctrines, including Buddhism, are meant to be used *by people*. Beware of them taking on a life of their own and *using* us. Remember the story of the monks and the beautiful woman who needed to cross the river, which I told you earlier.

'The importance of compassion in Buddhism cannot be overstated. Genuine compassion contains both wisdom and loving kindness – qualities we have been practising throughout this course.

'Compassion means having the aspiration for others to be free from suffering. We have to understand the nature of suffering and feel deep intimacy and empathy with all other sentient beings, and this happens naturally as we follow the practices, as I have been describing to you.

'But to come back to your question about abortion, Tim', he says, looking toward the tall doctor, who has a serious expression on his face.

'When you apply true compassion – wisdom and loving kindness – to the subject of abortion, you think of the suffering of the woman concerned; the desperation that causes some women – in places where abortion is still illegal – to try all kinds of painful, unsterile, unsafe procedures to induce an abortion – and sometimes even to commit suicide, such is their mental agony.

'And you may also think of the possible suffering of that baby, coming into the world when it is not wanted, when raising it would be a struggle for the mother, a burden on the family'.

The monk pauses, then says, quietly, 'And when you have experienced the reality of the Third Noble Truth, of cessation, and the reality of the oneness of everything – that oneness that is like a great ocean from which we rise up like a tiny ripple when we incarnate and to which we return when we leave our physical body, you begin to look at things in a different way.

'That is not to say that killing anything – anything at all – is what we would wish to do, but sometimes it is the most compassionate and loving choice. And compassion and love always, always, *always* come before doctrine.

'So always go back to this, and to mindfulness. Be in awareness. Find that place of No-self. All is peace, clarity, love and joy there. That is your true home. That is who you truly are. That is where you come from and to where you will return, as will any living being – though in reality we've never left it.

'We have just forgotten our true self that has become hidden by the ego structure we have – ironically – built to protect us. When you consider things from this perspective outside the ego-structure, instead of from the viewpoint of being imprisoned within it, you get a different take on life and its problems.

'The more you get into this space of awareness, the clearer things become. Go there – be there – often, and you will find that apparent contradictions fade away into the wholeness of life.'

The monk pauses and looks at Tim. 'Does that answer your question?' he asks.

'Yes, it does. Thank you', replies Tim, quietly.

'It's not up to anyone, any human being at all, to make moral judgments or to criticize another', says the monk.

There is silence for a moment, then Pam speaks. 'I teach English Literature', she says, 'and what you have just said reminds me of a well-known quote from the book that I've been teaching to one of my classes. In *To Kill a Mocking Bird,* Atticus says "You never really know a man until you stand in his shoes and walk around in them". We just can't judge another person, can we?'

'Quite so, quite so,' says the monk. He pauses thoughtfully, then continues, 'We live in a material world and sometimes there is no clear or perfect action. When you look "out there" many things are imperfect but when you look "in here"', he says, touching his heart, 'when you look at things from a spiritual perspective, they become clearer. I would advise you to look inside first. Get your own thoughts right.

'Act from your centre of peace, with loving kindness and mindfulness, treating others as you yourself would like to be treated. Be pure in your own thoughts and honest in your own dealings, and the rest will follow. Always remember that action follows intention.

'But – don't be attached to perfection', he adds, with a laugh.

There is another pause, then Suzi asks, 'Could we talk about sex?'

There's a stunned silence. Really, that woman is irrepressible. Then we all laugh, including the monk.

'I mean, the Buddha's attitude to sex', adds Suzi, quickly, blushing slightly.

'I know what you mean', says the monk, 'you're wondering how we interpret the Buddha's words "not misusing sex", aren't you?

'Yes', replies Suzi.

'Well', says the monk, 'think of it from the karmic point of view. The reason the Buddha gave us these guidelines in the Eightfold Path was to enable us to live in a way that would not embroil us in unnecessary karmic entanglements.

'And how does karma arise? Karma means action, and any action we make sets up a momentum and returns to us. So sexual acts that damage or cause pain to another would come into this category.

'In fact, the Buddha did give more detailed guidance on this. He said that "misusing" sex meant having sex with "those under the protection of their father, mother, brother, sister, relatives or clan; or of their religious community; or with those promised to someone else, protected by law and even with those betrothed."

The monk pauses, then turns to Suzi. 'Does that answer your question?'

'Yes, thank you', she says.

Then Dan says 'So the Buddha did not condemn homosexuality?'

'No, he did not', responds the monk. 'Sex is sex as far as the Buddha is concerned. He was quite matter-of-fact about it. He accepted that sexuality, like anger, greed and violence, is part of our physical nature, part of being human. As such, he did not judge these aspects of being human in a moral way, but he also said that we absolutely do not have to be a slave to them.

'And why is that?' asks the monk rhetorically. 'Because they are forms of desire', he answers himself. 'And attachment to desire causes suffering, as we have discovered. The Buddha has shown us how to let our attachment to desire go, as we have been saying throughout this course.

'But it does not mean that if you follow the Buddha's teaching you have to abstain from sex – that is, sex that does not harm anyone else. However, it does mean that you notice any attachment you have to it, just as you notice attachment to desire for food, money, success, ideals and ideas, and so on. These are desires that disrupt your inner peace and happiness and can control you, rather than you being in the driver's seat.

'I seem to have gone back to the car metaphor again', he adds, laughing.

'Of course, for us monks, it's altogether stricter. Our *vinaya*, the monastic precepts that we take when we are ordained, preclude any sexual activity whatsoever. We have to be absolutely celibate and sex-free, and the Buddha was very firm about this. He saw it as a necessity in order to attain enlightenment.'

'Why is that?' asks Maurice.

'Because having the possibility of sex – or possessions, or money or any other want stimulates the desires, and our training is all about freeing ourselves from the imprisonment of desire (as well as hatred, greed, clinging and craving). As I have said before, it's not wise or helpful to keep stirring them up; it doesn't help us to find inner peace.'

The monk stops and thinks for a moment. 'It's the same for non-monastics, for all of us,' he says. 'If you are trying to lose weight, you don't keep biscuits and chocolate in the house, do you? In the same way, if you are serious about practising the Eightfold Path, you do not put unnecessary temptation in your way – stimulating your passions with violent or sexually explicit books or films, for example. It's just common sense, really.'

There is another pause, then Suzi asks, 'Is the "no sex" vow a difficult one to keep?'

'Some monks really struggle with it', replies the monk. 'For others it is less challenging. But it's like anything else: when you accept it and give your mind to it – to being celibate, that is – it gets easier.'

The monk thinks for a moment, then says, 'I have not been a monk all my life, you know. I have had my moments and I can assure you, there's no sex in the world that gets close to the bliss of *nirvana*.'

He pauses, then adds with a chuckle 'or so I am told.'

When he says this, I remember something I read: that ordained Buddhist monks are not allowed to boast in any way about what spiritual states they may have attained.

The monk looks around and says: 'If we've completed our discussion on this, let's go on to Right Livelihood.'

Right Livelihood

'Right Livelihood means earning a living in a way that does not harm others, which enables us to put into practice the five precepts I just mentioned. So that is a living that does not involve killing, stealing, misusing sex, lying or abusing intoxicants. Or, as the Buddha said, "A lay follower should not engage in five types of business. Business in weapons, business in human beings, business in meat, business in intoxicants and business in poison.'"

'Does that mean it's wrong to do part-time work in a bar or to work in a butcher's?' asks Ed.

'Or on the deli counter in the supermarket?' asks Pam. 'I mean, how far do we have to take these things, especially these days when the economy is so difficult. Most of us are grateful just to have a job.'

'Quite so', responds the monk, 'and gratitude is a fine emotion. Being grateful for what we have eases pain and sadness, opens our heart and brings more good things into our life', he adds.

'The fact of the matter is, we do what we have to do, with mindfulness and loving kindness. We get on with life. We act with integrity, we keep our word, we never take what is not given; we don't indulge in scandal and gossip; we behave with compassion and loving kindness toward all living beings.

'That's a great basis – and takes a bit of doing, doesn't it? But when we behave like that, do you know what? We tend to attract the right circumstances into our life.

'So, do your best to behave impeccably, in whatever circumstances you find yourself. Be grateful for what you already have and expect better things to come.' He pauses. 'But don't be attached to them, of course', he adds with a laugh.

'You know, one can argue about moral dilemmas until one is blue in the face. We have to accept, as I said before, that this is an imperfect and impermanent world, and not pay *too* much attention to it. Concentrate on your inner world: on the peace and joy and love you find in your mindfulness meditation and work from this basis.

'Always act in accordance with your inner integrity. Do what feels right to you. As the Buddha says, it's all up to us, there's no one telling us what to do. "No one saves us but ourselves", the Buddha said. "No one can, and no one may. We ourselves must walk the path. Work out your own salvation. Do not depend on others."

'And, I add to that – be happy! Flow with life. Accept things as they are; don't kick unnecessarily against them.

'I'm reminded of something that happened to my teacher, Ajahn Sumedho.' He continues, 'When Ajahn Sumedho was a monk in Thailand he became very worried about the condition of the monastery, the discipline of the monks and what he felt was the general decline of the place.

'He has described how he could not understand why the Abbot, the Venerable Ajahn Chah, did nothing about it, did not discipline the monks and whip things into shape. Eventually, having brooded about it all for some time and got himself into a state of real upset, he went to Ajahn Chah and told him all the things that were wrong. And Ajahn Chah listened quietly and patiently, then simply said "Oh Sumedho, you do suffer a lot. It will change." And it did.

'Sometimes you just have to let things be for a time, knowing that they will eventually change. Sometimes we have to learn to accept life and not to take ourselves so seriously; sometimes when things are really difficult, and we've done all we possibly can, surrender is the only thing left to do. And sometimes, in an amazing way, the very act of surrender starts to put things right.'

The monk pauses, and smiles. 'You know', he says, 'I have just realized that in that little story about Sumedho we have an example of the power of mindfulness and the first three Noble Truths in action: be with the situation as it is right now; notice it but don't judge it; accept and embrace it – surrender the worry, as it were – and then it will cease.

'Try it on your own worries, and watch as the magical power of mindfulness works and transforms your life.

The monk pauses, then he comments, 'We have covered a great deal today, but before we go, let's join together in a few minutes of mindfulness, and focus this time on how the body-scan meditation can be used for pain relief.

'This can be so effective that it is being used in some medical practices. But whether or not you have any aches and pains at present, it is always a helpful exercise, so let's go through the process.

'In fact,' he says with a laugh, 'it's very good to practise using mindfulness for pain relief when you simply have little aches and pains, so that you can do it easily and naturally if and when you need it for bigger pains.

'You can go through a full body scan or you can just focus on the particular area that is hurting, which is what we will do today.

'If you haven't got any aches and pains, just put your mindfulness on your whole body and any parts that might be tense.'

Meditation For Pain Relief

'Gently close your eyes.

'Become aware of your breathing: of the air flowing in through your nostrils, going down into your lungs, then releasing through your nostrils. Take a few beautiful, healing breaths.

'Bring your awareness to any part of the body where there is pain or discomfort. Open yourself to the feelings of pain. At this moment, there is awareness of pain: there is suffering. Breathe steadily …

'Accept the pain and suffering exactly as it is. Release resistance: fears, anger, impatience, guilt or any other thoughts or emotions you may have. Allow them to slip away.

'At this moment, there is suffering, just suffering. Allow the suffering to be. If you can, embrace the suffering. Say, "Welcome suffering. I welcome you into my heart. I accept you."

'There is suffering, but you are not the suffering. There is the suffering and there is the part of you viewing the suffering, part of your mind that is aware of the suffering, but is not suffering.

'Rest in this part of you. Sink into the security, the absolute security of this "awareness" part of you. Feel the peace; feel the love.

'Say to yourself, "May I be free from fear. May I be well. May I be happy, exactly as I am. May I be safe and at ease."'

'Breathe and drink in the peace, the healing. It is as it is and all is well.'

I am feeling a little tired, though I do not think I have any specific aches and pains. But when I really think about my body, I realize my jaw is very tense and my shoulders are rather hunched. Also my neck is quite stiff. I decide to focus on these parts of my body.

I settle into the meditation; I love it. I can see how helpful it could be for real pain. I wonder to myself whether it would help the excruciating migraines that I get sometimes. I will try it next time, though maybe with my new practice of meditation, I won't get any.

'So', the monk is saying, 'that is a pain-relief meditation. There is one important thing to remember: remain "in the moment", without attachment to outcomes. But the more you practise it on little aches and pains, the more familiar it will become and the more easily you will be able to apply it any time you need to.

'More of the Buddha's medicine?' laughs Suzi.

'Yes, indeed', says the monk, 'the Buddha's very best: *metta* and mindfulness combined.'

He pauses for a moment and looks around the group. 'There has been quite a lot to take in today. Next time we will consider the final group of qualities that makes up the Eightfold Path', he says.

'Treat yourselves gently; be kind to yourselves.' He pauses, then chuckles, 'That reminds me of something that the Dalai Lama said, something that always makes me smile, "Be kind whenever possible. It is always possible."'

We all smile and laugh a little, then we join together in a short chant, pick up our things, and go out into the warm early-evening sunshine.

Quick Review

- Certain actions bring about certain results, sometimes known as karma.
- In Right Action, Right Speech and Right Livelihood, the Buddha gave details of speech and behaviour that will bring positive results or good karma. He summarised it in the Five Precepts:
  - No killing
  - No stealing
  - No misusing sex
  - No lying
  - No abusing intoxicants
- Act from mindfulness with integrity, and behave with compassion and loving kindness toward all living beings, treating others as you would like to be treated yourself.
- Be pure in your thoughts and honest in your dealings. Keep your word, don't indulge in scandal and gossip and only take what is given to you.

Practice

- Reflect on Right Speech and Right Action and how far you can express them in your own life. Perhaps work on one aspect of your life that you can bring into line with the Buddha's teaching.

- Make the intention to be kind to yourself. Remember, 'A jug fills drop by drop.'
- Get into the habit of pausing and taking a mindful breath or two for a moment before speaking or acting.
- Meditate each day for 20 minutes.
  - Continue with your *metta* practice at the end of your meditation, starting with yourself as usual, and then your patron or benefactor. Then add someone you love, such as your partner or child. Say to yourself: 'May I be safe. May I be happy. May I be well and at ease.' Then picture your patron and say, 'May you be well. May you be happy. May you be safe and at ease'. Finally, imagine your loved one and say, 'May you be well. May you be happy. May you be safe and at ease'.

Week 7

Inner Peace, Outer Peace

The weather has broken. After a beautiful hot spell we had a big thunderstorm last night and now the rain is pouring down. People arrive for our meeting looking rather bedraggled. Sam looks really wet, his glasses all steamed up, sandy-coloured hair dripping. He puts his waterproofs in our utility room; I give him a towel to dry his face.

I decide to put the central heating on – I know, crazy for July, but this is Britain! Sam sits with his back against one of the radiators, warming up.

But despite the heating, I'm still feeling quite chilly and I ask the monk whether we may start with a cup of tea. I am not sure what the monastic etiquette is about this, but he seems to like the idea.

'You put the kettle on and it can be heating while we do our opening ceremony', he says, 'then we can start with a recap and questions while we drink our tea.'

So that is what we do. I pop quickly out into the kitchen, accompanied by Maggie who has offered to help me. We fill two electric kettles to the brim, half-fill my largest saucepan with water, hunt out some tea bags and a couple of big trays, then return to the group, who are now sitting quietly waiting for us.

We put our hands into prayer position and bow our head to the monk. I'm learning, but it still feels unnatural to me. It does help to know that I am bowing in gratitude for the teaching and those who have brought it to us by practising it and passing it on down through the centuries, rather than bowing in deference to some deity. But I do still feel a bit self-conscious.

The monk waits for a moment or two until we are all still, then he performs the usual ceremony, lighting the candles and the incense stick, and we open with a chant. I enjoy the chanting these days. We do it in Pali, with a translation running alongside it on our chanting sheets, so we know roughly what we are saying.

But I really like the sound of the words for their own sake, and the feeling of unity within the group as we all join in. I also realize that chanting is very helpful for mindfulness; being totally at one with the sound as we make it is rather like being at one with the breath. I think I would like to do a bit more chanting. I remember reading some years ago that Tina Turner said that Buddhism – and particularly the chanting – had saved and transformed her life. And now I'm beginning to understand why.

As the chant ends, Maggie and I slip quietly out into the kitchen, make a big pot of 'builders' tea remembering that this is the monk's choice, and put hot water and the packets of assorted teas on to the tray, along with disposable cups and both soya and cow's milk.

As we walk down the hall toward the sitting room we hear chatter and a burst of laughter – it sounds more like a party than a meditation class. I wonder what they are talking about.

I make a point of offering the monk his cup of tea, knowing that he is not allowed to take anything unless it is clearly given to him. The rest of the group, assisted by Maggie, help themselves to their preferred drinks.

'So', says the monk, smiling around, we have been considering the Eightfold Path, the way of life that the Buddha described for a happy life – or maybe that should be "prescribed", he says, laughing, and looking at Dr Tim, who smiles.

'Yes', he continues, 'It was – and is – a prescription to free us from pain and suffering. Just as a doctor's treatment may include advice – or instructions – regarding our diet and way of life in addition to the medication, so does the Buddha's teaching through the Eightfold Path.

'As we have already discovered, this covers all areas of life: mental, physical and emotional. We need all the teaching – the mindfulness and the guidance for living in the world as expressed in the Four Noble Truths and the Eightfold Path – in order to get the fullest benefit.

'So we have already looked at the first five principles in the Eightfold Path, those that are related to our minds: Right View and Right Intention; and those connected with our physical life: Right Speech, Right Action and Right Livelihood. Now we come to the last group of qualities, the ones that we can think of as corresponding to the heart – qualities that contribute toward our emotional stability. These are Right Effort, Right Mindfulness and Right Concentration. And I must remind you that although they're listed sixth, seventh and eighth, it does not mean that they are any less important than the ones that precede them.

'As I have said before, we are not thinking in a linear way here. All the qualities work together. Practising this last group, Right

Effort, Right Mindfulness and Right Concentration, brings us the mental and emotional development and stability that enable us to develop true wisdom through our experience. And thus we arrive back at the beginning of the Eightfold Path, with wisdom or Right View, as we call it.

'So today we will consider Right Effort, Right Mindfulness and Right Concentration, one by one.

Right Effort

'Right Effort. What does that mean? Well, it really means exactly what it says: doing our best.

'So where do we start?' the monk chuckles, then adds: 'The Buddha gives us some guidance on this. He said there are four aspects to Right Effort. These are:

- preventing negative states of mind such as greed, hatred and delusion from arising.
- releasing those that have already arisen.
- cultivating what the Buddha referred to as "skilful" qualities, such as loving kindness, generosity and wisdom.
- strengthening the "skilful" qualities we already have.

'Now, with the first part of this, preventing negative qualities such as greed, hatred, and delusion from arising, and releasing those that we already have, we're back to what we learned in the

First and Second Noble Truths. We notice when such negative thoughts come up and – then what? What do we do?'

The monk pauses and looks around the group. He waits for a moment – we are all silent – and then he says, 'We experience these thoughts or feelings within us; we don't try to change them. We let them be and then, through letting them be, we let them go. Remember: observe them, let them be and let them go.

'Let negative thoughts go; let go of hurts, let go of resentment. Remember the story of the Buddha and the angry man? It's the same thing with insults: they don't belong to you unless you accept them; and if you don't accept them, they continue to belong to the person who "offered" them to you.

'In any case, who are you hurting when you hold on to anger and resentment? You're certainly not hurting the other person or changing the situation. You're hurting yourself. It's a bit like what the Buddha said about anger, do you know the quote?'

The monk stops but no one speaks, so he himself replies, 'The Buddha said, "Holding on to anger is like grasping a hot coal with the intention of throwing it at someone else; you are the one who gets burned". It's the same with taking offence about something. You are the one who gets hurt.

'And retaliation gets you nowhere, it just perpetuates the anger or the insult.'

The monk pauses, then says, 'What we all need to do is to stop that cycle of pain. There is a way. Do you know what that is?'

No one speaks.

'It's forgiveness', he explains. 'Forgiveness is the most beautiful, healing emotion you can feel. When you've been hurt, let that hurt go; let your heart be empty of hurt and harm, so that it can be filled with – flooded with – the cleansing, purifying quality of forgiveness.

'Those who forgive are the strong ones. When you can forgive another and feel your heart fill with the healing balm of peace and joy that follows forgiveness, *you* are the powerful one, the one feeling the bliss. If only everyone could realize this. If everyone practised forgiveness, the world would be healed overnight.'

'Huh, I wish!' comments Ed, 'That's quite a simplistic view.'

Oh my goodness! Ed's at it again – he always seems to be challenging the monk.

'I mean', he adds quickly, 'you make it all sound so simple – finding happiness, healing the world.'

The monk smiles and replies, 'The prescription – the medicine for peace and happiness, both individually and for the world – *is* simple: it's *taking* the medicine that is the problem.'

He chuckles, thinks for a moment, then smiles and says 'There's a nice little story about this. Would you like to hear it?

'Once upon a time, so the story goes, an old king went to visit a wise hermit who lived in a house – a nest – in a tree, as hermits often did in those days. The king had a question, "What is the most important part of the Buddha's teaching?" he asked.

The hermit thought for a while, then answered: "Do no evil. Do only good. Purify your heart." The king, in view of his eminence and the great effort he had made to reach the hermit in this obscure place, was expecting to hear a long, wise discourse. He couldn't believe his ears. "But even a child can understand that!" he blustered.

There was another pause, then the hermit replied, "Yes, and even an 80-year-old man cannot do it".'

We all laugh, including the monk, who adds: 'But there is a serious point there. In many ways the Buddha's teaching *is* simple. It's down-to-earth, designed for ordinary people – the people the Buddha was meeting all the time – the poor, the sick, the sad, the suffering; people with no education, no money, no hope – that's why he made it so clear and easy to understand.

'And if you follow the Buddha's teaching, it works. In fact, it is deceptively simple, because the more you practise it, the more you realize how profound it is.'

The monk pauses reflectively, then adds, 'And the point I'm making is that it *is* simple – simple enough for a five-year-old to practise – but you have to *do* it. Just *do* it. Make a difference.

'Practise what we have just been talking about – Right Effort – by really making an effort. What are you waiting for? Life is short, the need is great. Just do it. Change your life – and every life that changes for the better, changes the world. That is a fact.'

There is silence. I think that's the most forceful I've ever heard the monk speak. It certainly makes me resolve to try harder. It's easy to put things off, to let things slide, to be 'too busy'. I resolve to try harder.

'There's a lot to remember', comments Suzi.

Yes, I know there is', says the monk, kindly. 'But as we said before, if you make the intention really seriously, action follows.'

'I find it quite hard to remember it all, too', adds Debbie.

'You remember what I said earlier?' responds the monk. 'One of the things that attracted me most to Theravada Buddhism?'

No one speaks. He's said so much, I can't think exactly what he is talking about.

'The postcard?' asks Dan.

'Yes!' says the monk, happily, smiling broadly. 'Apart from the fact that I really liked the idea of a philosophy for life that no one was trying to thrust down my throat, one that I could test out for myself and discover the validity – or not – of it for myself, one of the things that attracted me to Buddhism at the beginning, and still does, was the fact that the core of the whole teaching is so simple and succinct that it can be written on a postcard.

'I think I am going to do just that', says Suzi. 'Maybe it's the teacher in me, but I am going to write them out on a postcard and keep it in my bag. I think I might make a poster, too, and put it up in my kitchen – perhaps of the Eightfold Path.'

'What a good idea!' I exclaim, visualizing a colourful poster.

'Or you could put it into one of your electronic devices', suggests Sam, 'by making a screensaver, or add it into your reminders on your phone.'

'What excellent ideas!' agrees the monk. 'And when you've done that' he continues, chuckling, 'just get on and *do it* – put the teaching into practice moment by moment. And the more you do it, the easier it will get because it will become a habit.'

'They say if you do something for three weeks it becomes a habit and then you keep on doing it', says Suzi.

'I'm not sure about the three weeks', says the monk, 'and I wouldn't put a time on it. Just do it, bit by bit. Make the intention; take the first step – and then simply keep on stepping.'

The monk adds: 'And remember your *metta* practice. Be kind to yourself. Find ways to support yourself in your practice; organize your way of life to make it easy for you to follow the Eightfold Path. Be practical. Keep away from things that make it hard to follow the precepts. That's what we do in the monastery, as I mentioned before.

'Isn't that cheating, though?' asks Ed. 'Isn't it easier not to do something if the temptation is not there?'

The monk laughs. 'No, Ed, it's not particularly easy, especially at first. But it all depends how you want to use your energy. If you want to use it fighting the temptation that is all around you, so be it. But if you would rather use your energy for other things, for *living*, for meditation, for joy, then support yourself by keeping your surroundings pure and free from things that will arouse in you the five foes: greed, hate, delusion, clinging and craving'.

'But to come back to what we were saying, habit does build day by day. Think how people can give up smoking. It's a combination of intention and what we have been talking about, effort – Right Effort, if you like', he adds, merrily. 'And if the cigarettes aren't there, it's easier not to smoke – that's just being practical.

'But that's enough about effort. Let's move on to the next quality, the penultimate one, Right Mindfulness.'

Right Mindfulness

'So here we are back again with mindfulness, the very first quality we learned about when we started this course. It's also one of the "twin pillars of Buddhism": the two "m"s, mindfulness and *metta*.

'We will come back to *metta*, but now let us consider once again the quality of Right Mindfulness. Since the very beginning of our study we have been learning about mindfulness and I know that many of you have been practising it, both as you go about your everyday life and in your daily meditation. Now we're reminded of it again in the Eightfold Path.'

There is a slight pause, then Maurice asks, 'So does the Eightfold Path really repeat the first three Noble Truths?'

'In a way, I suppose it does', answers the monk. 'As I said earlier, the Eightfold Path contains everything, so it does encompass the first three Noble Truths. It also focuses very much on how we can put the first three Noble Truths into practice in our everyday lives – when we are off the meditation mat and out in the world.'

The monk thinks for a moment, then adds, 'You see how interrelated it all is – it fits together so precisely. In fact, you only need half a postcard to write it on once you've got your head around it – well, certainly only one side!' he says, laughing. 'So, let's just remind ourselves of what mindfulness is.'

The monk asks, 'Would anyone like to say anything about the experience of mindfulness?'

He looks around the group. I wonder whether anyone is going to be brave enough to speak, then Suzi says, slightly hesitantly, 'Being mindful means bringing our attention to the present moment, doesn't it?'

'Yes', replies the monk, 'to *now*. It is being aware of what we are experiencing at this moment in our surroundings, our body, our breathing.'

'It is focusing on what is going on in this moment, isn't it?' agrees Nikki.

'Yes', answers the monk, 'and just noticing; accepting; letting be without commenting, criticizing, judging, wishing or comparing anything. It is noticing when we get caught in an increasing web of thoughts and simply bringing ourselves back to our breathing, to all that is in the present moment.'

'That happens often to me' says Sam, 'Getting caught in the web of thoughts, I mean. I think I've got a long way to go.'

There's a murmur of agreement from some of the other members of the group.

'Yes, it does take practice', says the monk, 'and like any other new skill that you are learning, you just have to make the intention to do it and to persevere. If you are persistent, you will find that it becomes more natural. Just keep noticing what is going on and bringing your mind back to the present moment.

There is a pause, then Gwyn comments, 'The thing I find so helpful about mindfulness is that it is something we can practise the whole time, whenever we think of it – for example, when we're washing up; working at the computer; walking along the pavement; waiting for a bus; or standing in a queue.'

'Yes', agrees the monk. 'It can become an ongoing part of our life, of who we are. And the more mindful we become, the more we experience the happiness, freedom and peace that is within us – and that is something anyone can experience for themselves very early in the practice of mindfulness. It is a real incentive for keeping going.'

The monk looks around the group. We are all silent, perhaps wondering how long it will take for mindfulness to become such a natural habit, and resolving to try harder.

'So, are there any more questions about mindfulness?' the monk asks.

When no one replies, he says, 'Then let us move on to the final principle, Right Concentration.'

Right Concentration

'What does Right Concentration mean? It's really about focus. It's encouraging us to keep on with our mindfulness, with our meditation. It's a strengthening of our resolve to put into practice all of the qualities of the Eightfold Path. It means keeping our mind and our intention focused on what we are doing.' The monk pauses.

We are quiet, trying to get our minds around the significance of his words, then Debbie says, reflectively, 'It's quite hard to concentrate sometimes, isn't it? I find that challenging. There are so many distractions.'

'Yes', agrees Joan, 'especially with all this Internet stuff – and twittering or whatever it's called.'

'"Tweeting", I think it's called tweeting' says Rodney, correcting his wife.

'Whatever it's called', she says, 'there is so much to distract us that it's hard to keep focused, especially for the young people.'

'Yes', agrees the monk. 'Right Concentration is almost deeper than that. It's a bit like setting an intention – we have to get into the right mindset, particularly making our mind still, and letting go of conditions and thoughts that disrupt the mind. It can be done.'

The monk thinks for a moment, then adds, 'The Buddha identified and described the attitudes of mind that disrupt concentration and mindfulness. He listed them and called them the Five Hindrances.'

Before he can continue, Suzi interrupts, commenting, 'The Buddha did like his numbers, didn't he! Four Noble Truths, Eightfold Path, Five Precepts and now Five Hindrances.'

'Oh, we haven't really even started yet!' replies the monk, chuckling. 'There are many, many more: Three Refuges, Five Aggregates, Ten Perfections, Ten Fetters, Twelve Links of

Dependent Arising, and so on. There are lots more numbered categories.

'You have to remember that when the Buddha was teaching 2,500 years ago in the forests of northern India, nothing could be written down. So he spoke in ways that could be remembered: numbers, groups of items, alliteration, a great deal of repetition. That's how his teachings came to be passed down for two or three centuries, until they could be written down.

'And it's also how we have managed to get such pure teaching direct from the Buddha, almost as though he were speaking to us today.'

The monk continues, 'But we don't have to get complicated. As I said at the beginning of this course, the Four Noble Truths contain all we really need for living. However, these other groups of conditions and categories can be useful to contemplate at some point to shed further light on our development or on life in general. The Five Hindrances that I just mentioned are a case in point. They comprise a list of things that can impede or hinder our development.

'Just for your interest and so that you can look out for them in yourself – and we all get them – the Five Hindrances are:

- sensual desire – the craving for pleasure of the senses
- anger and feelings of ill-will and hate
- boredom and being half-hearted about what we are doing – the Buddha referred to this as "sloth-torpor"

- restlessness and worry
- doubt – lack of conviction or trust

'To achieve Right Concentration, we have to let go of these five conditions when they arise.'

'And how do we do that?' asks Tim.

As I mentioned, it starts with intention', says the monk. 'Use your willpower to intend that you will be able to concentrate. Intention is powerful, as we have already said. But also, knowing what the Five Hindrances are enables you to arrange your life so that you can be as free from them as possible. For example, when you want to meditate and concentrate, avoid having things around that stimulate your desires or, for that matter, arouse hate within you.'

'Oh right', says Suzi, 'that means no more television or radio news for me – or even too much reading of the newspapers because they always make me hate politicians – and that's not good for my concentration.'

Everyone laughs.

'Quite so, quite so,' replies the monk. 'I certainly wouldn't advise listening to the news before you want to meditate or last thing at night before you go to sleep, either.

'Be aware of the sensitivity of your mind and feelings to external stimuli and make your own environment as calm, loving and harmonious as you can. This will help you to find inner peace.

'And always bring your mind back to the present moment. That is the most important thing. If you develop that ability – and, believe me, you can; everyone can – then you can be at peace anywhere, any time, any place; you don't need to depend on external circumstances.

'No matter what is going on outside, you always have control over your "inner climate", as we have been saying throughout this course. But it's good when you have both inner and outer peace. Like everything else, it all works together; inner peace brings more outer peace, and outer peace makes it easier for you to find inner peace and to have Right Concentration.'

Ed puts up his hand.

'Yes, Ed?' asks the monk, smiling kindly at him.

Ed flushes slightly. It's a different Ed from the one who cheekily – or maybe jokily – likes to challenge the monk. He's looking a bit pale, a bit concerned.

'My problem', he says rather haltingly, 'is anger. I find I get angry so easily. I realize that's very much against the Buddha's teaching, and since I've been doing this course I've become more aware of it and I'd like to know how I can get rid of it.'

The monk smiles. 'I understand about anger', he says. 'It is something I have struggled with, too. A monastic life does not isolate you from feelings of anger or any of the other negative emotions such as hate, jealousy, fear and so on, you know.

'We all experience them because they are part of being human. 'But your question is interesting. Notice what you said,

"*I* get angry so easily. *My* problem is anger. How can *I get rid of* it? That's what we all want to do, isn't it – get rid of bad feelings. So, what do you do?

'The first thing is to get 'I' out of the situation. Instead of saying 'I get angry', and thinking of it as 'my problem', try saying 'there is anger'. Become the observer of the anger – remember? How does that make you feel? Notice how that puts a bit of space between you and the anger. You're not owning it; it doesn't belong to you; it is simply anger.

'It is human nature to experience anger; it is part of the state of being human. But by noticing the anger – by saying to ourselves 'there is anger' – we are doing two things. First, we are admitting that the anger is there – we're not saying, "Angry? What do you mean, angry? I'm not angry!" between clenched teeth. We are admitting the anger. And second, we are de-personalizing the anger. We are making a bit of space between it and us; we are viewing it and becoming detached from it.

'When we do these two things – admitting the anger and de-personalizing it – we immediately feel more peaceful. Instead of being completely caught up in an emotion that is out of our control, we find ourselves in the position of being the *observer* of the anger.

'Then we need to keep our observation clean, to watch that we do not add extra layers on top of the anger by blaming others for "making" us angry, or by blaming ourselves and feeling guilty for being angry.

'Keep focusing on "there is anger" – or "there is suffering", if you prefer to say that. Feel it inside you, but let it be. You could even try Ajahn Sumedho's trick of saying "welcome, anger", but that's asking a lot at first. If you persevere with this approach you *will* reach that stage of being able to say "welcome" to the anger, and feel it dissolve. And what a lovely feeling of true power and control that will give you!"

'I can't imagine ever being like that', says Ed, wistfully.

'Yes, truly, it will come if you put in the work', says the monk encouragingly. 'Start with minor irritations to get yourself into the habit of welcoming anger and other uncomfortable feelings. This method works with them all, as you'll see. Peace will come.

'Remember, too, what we have been saying about our feelings being transitory. They come, they go. Anger can rise up in a flash and then it can pass just as quickly. Anger is like a dark storm cloud – or perhaps a flash of lightning – some stormy weather that comes into your inner landscape, and like any weather, it passes. All our storms and dark clouds pass. Our natural state inside is sunny – always remember, the sun will shine again.

'When you feel anger or, for that matter, any other passion arising, try to pause long enough to allow yourself to observe it. Don't let it push you into immediate speech or action. Take at least one deep breath – and if you can make it a mindfulness breath, which you will be able to do with practice – so much the better.'

'Or you could try counting up to ten, like my Nan used to tell me', suggests Debbie.

Pam puts up her hand and the monk invites her to speak.

'Is it helpful', she asks, 'to thump a pillow or to go outside and have a good scream?'

'That can feel helpful at the time', replies the monk, 'and it's better to thump a pillow than to hit a person or kick a dog, but really you're just encouraging the anger when you do this.

'For true inner peace and freedom, you need to go through the stages I've described: admit the anger to yourself, observe the anger without bringing in any other confusing thoughts of blame or guilt and then you will find you can accept it, let it be and let it go.

'Don't try to get rid of it. If you do what I've described, it will dissolve of its own accord – like those storm clouds – and every time those buttons get pressed, the anger will have a little less hold on you.'

Nikki looks doubtful. 'I really hate myself for being angry', she says.

'That's simply adding another layer of pain on top of the anger, isn't it?' replies the monk kindly. 'It's beating yourself up. Just focus on the feeling of anger inside you. Acknowledge it; welcome it if you can and let it be. Stop all the inner thoughts of blame and guilt. Be kind and accepting of yourself and your anger. Give yourself – and your anger – some *metta*.'

The monk pauses, then says, 'That reminds me of an ancient Buddhist story about an anger-eating demon. Would you like to hear it?'

There is a murmur of affirmation from the group.

'The demon', says the monk, 'survived by eating anger and as he lived among humans, he always had plenty of food.'

The group laughs.

The monk continues, 'And if ever he began to run short, he just aggravated people and made them do things that would stir up anger in other people and cause wars. One day he got rather above himself and thought he'd have a change of diet, so he used his magic powers to transfer himself to the realms of the gods and the palace of a king god called Sakka.

'The king happened to be away from his palace at the time, so the demon marched straight in and sat down on his throne.

'When the gods came into the throne room and saw the demon sitting there, they couldn't believe their eyes. They shouted at the demon, cursing and reviling him, screaming at him to get off the throne and go away. But the demon was gorging himself on their anger, getting fatter and fatter, bigger and bigger. The gods did not know what to do.

'Then, all of a sudden, the King Sakka returned. He was wise and enlightened, perfectly poised – he had obviously learned the processes for dealing with anger that we have been talking about today – and he was at peace within himself.

"Welcome, friend!" he said to the demon, as his courtiers looked on, amazed and aghast. "I hope you are comfortable? Is there anything else you need? Can I get you a drink? What would you like?"

'King Sakka continued to talk to the demon in this kind and welcoming way and as he did so, the demon began to shrink. He got smaller and smaller and smaller, until the king was able to scoop him up in his hand and take him outside.'

The monk chuckles. 'I like to think of that story when I feel angry', he comments. 'It shows so clearly how anger feeds on itself. Anger begets anger. But when we bring in some loving kindness to ourselves, the anger starts to shrink.

'So, that is a long-winded way of saying be kind and loving to yourself. Accept the anger; show love toward yourself, which will heal the pain that caused the anger in the first place and you'll find the anger will shrink away and disappear.'

There is a pause while the group reflects on this, then Debbie asks, 'Does the same thing happen with depression? I have heard that mindfulness meditation can help to alleviate depression.'

'Yes', replies the monk. 'Mindfulness meditation – what we have been doing throughout this course – has been shown to be very helpful. Sitting with your eyes closed, focusing on your breath going in and out, in and out; noticing what is going on in your body; coming back to your beautiful, healing breath; and when thoughts arise, letting them go... all this is very beneficial.'

'Doing this for 20 to 30 minutes a day for eight weeks has been found to reduce the symptoms of depression. One of the challenges with depression is that we tend to brood, to go over and over things in our head. So training ourselves always to come back to the breath creates space in our head. It helps us to become the observer, rather than being caught up in all the fog of negative thoughts.

'We begin to find that "we" are not the thoughts; we begin to find a little space inside us. And the more we watch the breath, the bigger this space becomes. There is more freedom and peace within. The sun begins to break through the clouds.'

The monk pauses and looks around the room, then continues, 'You know, demons can feed on depression in the same way as they feed on anger. I'm speaking metaphorically here, of course, but depression – indeed, any negative emotion that we may be feeling – tends to feed on itself and increase in size.

'And the remedy is the same one as Sakka, the king of the gods, used: loving kindness. You can't have too much of it. Be kind and gentle to yourself. Treat yourself like the king treated the angry demon and watch the anger, depression or whatever the suffering is shrink until you can pick it up, just as the king picked up the shrunken demon. Then let it blow away in the wind, like a puff of smoke.'

The monk looks at the group. People are relaxed and smiling, and there is a feeling of friendliness and warmth among us. He smiles broadly

'So now', he says, 'we've looked at all Four Noble Truths, including each one of the principles of the Eightfold Path – your passport to paradise, to *nirvana*' he chuckles.

'No', replies Rodney, also laughing, 'I think it's more of a road map'.

'Or an instruction manual for life', adds Robert. 'If only we were all born with one!'

'In fact, we are', responds the monk, 'but unfortunately we do not realize it, and by the time we are old enough to understand this, we've lost some of the message.'

'What do you mean?' asks Pam, looking puzzled.

'It's in here', says the monk, pointing to his heart. 'When we are very young the building blocks of our ego have not yet been put in place, so we have easy access to that state of purity, joy and intimate connection with all living things, which is our natural state of being. It is natural for us to be open and trusting, as well as spontaneous in our actions and reactions. We follow our inner voice of true guidance – the voice that urges us to be loving and kind.

'If we are encouraged in this by sensitive and wise parents, we can keep the channel open for longer, but most of us soon lose this open-hearted approach as we learn to protect ourselves from pain by building up our ego.'

'That's very interesting', says Debbie. 'Could you tell us more about how to raise children?'

Now, there's a big question!' replies the monk, with a chuckle.

'But to give a few pointers, by finding your own centre of peace and living your own life according to the Four Noble Truths to the best of your ability, you are already giving any child a great start in life.

'Children absorb the atmosphere and conditions around them

like little sponges and nothing is more harmonious for a child than to be brought up in a home where there is peace, love and a code of ethics to guide them to behave in ways that will not bring suffering to themselves or others.

'Then, make time to listen to them. Be there for them; listen to them – to their fears, their hopes, their problems – without judgment. Oh, how freeing is that? To know that we can pour out our hearts without fear of criticism or being told what we "should" or "should not" do, just safe in the security of the love that surrounds us.

'Listen – and love.' The monk pauses. 'Come to think of it, that's a good mantra for all relationships, isn't it?

'You know', he adds thoughtfully, 'believing in someone – seeing through your children's pain and suffering to the potential within them, to their highest self, and encouraging them to see that, too, and to believe in themselves, is far more helpful than sympathy and compassion. Saying things like "Oh you poor thing, I'm so sorry" – that just encourages the negative view, doesn't it?

'Help them to believe in themselves, to be the very best that they can be. We do that by seeing within them, to what they want to be, to achieve, and treating them as if they already have. Belief in someone is very powerful.'

The monk pauses for a moment, then adds, 'We can do this with everyone, not just children. Thought is powerful – let us use it positively in our lives.'

'Is it good to teach a child to meditate?' asks Nikki.

'Mindfulness is a wonderful gift to teach a child', replies the monk.

'A little child can also be taught to be mindful when doing simple, everyday things like cleaning their teeth. But don't make heavy weather of it; don't make it a chore. Again, your child will take their cue from you. If you practise mindfulness naturally, then they will copy that.

'Help them to notice their breath; even to count as they breathe in and out. What a blessing to realize the comfort and healing of the breath at an early age!

'Holding a young child close to you, letting them breathe with you as you breathe while thinking of peace and healing, can be a beautiful way to introduce them to meditation and their own inner world.

'Doing a walking meditation with a child is also beneficial, especially if they are angry, worried or upset. Hold their hand and walk with them, feet firmly on the ground. Get them to breathe in, then breathe out steadily – that's so calming and uplifting.'

The monk pauses thoughtfully, then adds, 'It's helpful for children to know that sometimes they may feel sad or frightened, lonely or angry, and that this is normal. They can learn to deal with these feelings by noticing them and simply letting them be or even saying 'welcome' to them.

'When a child – or anyone else, for that matter – is sad or upset, it's tempting to say "there, there, it's all right", or to give them a sweet to "make it better", but it's much more helpful to encourage them to feel their feelings, accept them and let them be – just as we ourselves are learning to do. Then they can let them go and be free of them, rather than just papering over the cracks and building up a bank of inner pain that has to be dealt with in the future.

'When we're practising mindfulness, which can be such a wonderful tool for anyone at any age or stage in their life, there are a couple of things that we need to look out for. One is this tendency we all have to try and blot out the suffering from our minds; to distract ourselves by eating, drinking, even blotting it out by thinking "healing thoughts" – anything to put it out of our minds. This, too, can be simply a kind of papering over the cracks, which does not help.

'It's far better to be honest and notice and accept "there is suffering". Look at it and understand what it's about. There's always an attachment involved, so work away at it in your mind until you've discovered the attachment that's at the bottom of it. Then you'll feel a release of pressure inside you and the process of letting go will be on its way. Accept that the "letting go" is happening.

The monk stops for a moment to gather his thoughts, then adds, 'But without being attached to outcomes, of course. That's the second stumbling block, attachment to outcomes. We always want to fix things, don't we? But if we can just let them be – "surrender them to the universe, to the stream of life", they will work themselves out.

'Try to accept things and people exactly as they are without trying to change or fix anything. When we let go and let things be, we allow the universe to show us what is in store for us in our lives.'

'I find that rather challenging', says Rodney

'Being the control freak that you are!' chips in his wife, laughing.

Rodney goes silent.

The monk says kindly, 'I know – it takes practice. It's a big change from the way some people think about things, from the way we're conditioned to live our lives. But start with little things: accept little things about yourself. And accept the things in the world that you can't change, such as the government, the crimes people commit, the state of the national debt and so on – you know, little things', jokes the monk.

'You'll find that acceptance then becomes a state of mind quite quickly. And you know, Rodney – and this applies to everyone – you'll be amazed at the effect that this has on your own "inner climate".

'Not suffering all the time for the state of the world brings so much inner peace. And this will spread to your acceptance of the things that are going on in your own life. Little by little, peace will come.'

The monk pauses, then says: 'But coming back to children for a moment, I think the metaphor of "inner weather" can be useful to them. They can notice when the clouds – or storms even – arise and learn that if they wait, the sun will shine again. It's never too early to learn that you're in charge of your own inner "weather".

'We do these things with love and acceptance, not criticism or pressure on the children to be different from what they are. We are seeing them as the perfect, loving beings that they truly are.'

There's a sound of surprise from the group: 'Gosh, you should see my little terrors', says Ed.

Everyone laughs, but the monk persists. 'No, I'm serious. That is the way with relationships. We look through the ego, the house that has been constructed to protect against the pain and suffering of the world, "the slings and arrows of outrageous fortune", as Shakespeare put it. We see the love that is at the core and the hopes of what could-be and we help the child to develop their true potential by loving them and believing in them

'And we can do this with any relationship, any person. As we get in touch more and more with our own inner core, we open ourselves to the inner core of others. We see beneath the ego, through the layers of self-protective humour, world-weariness and sophistication to the dashed hopes, the uncertainty, the fears and disappointments that have led to the creation of the ego structure.

And we love what we sense at the heart of them for we know, deep down, that they are us and we are them. All ripples in the same ocean of life.'

There is silence. The monk pauses for a while, then asks, 'Do you understand? Do you get that?'

No one says anything, so the monk continues, 'As we take the Four Noble Truths to heart, as we think about suffering, we realize that whoever we are, wherever we are, we're all experiencing it. Shakespeare had a way of putting it in *The Merchant of Venice*. Do you remember? I had to learn Shylock's speech at school and I still remember it:

'"I am a Jew. Hath not a Jew eyes? Hath not a Jew hands, organs, dimensions, senses, affections, passions; fed with the same food, hurt with the same weapons, subject to the same diseases, heal'd by the same means, warm'd and cool'd by the same winter and summer, as a Christian is? If you prick us, do we not bleed? If you tickle us, do we not laugh? If you poison us, do we not die? And if you wrong us, do we not revenge? If we are like you in the rest, we will resemble you in that."

'Our true nature lies below all that ego stuff of race, religion, profession, outer appearance. It is the reality of our spirit within, it is *us*, the infinite ocean of which we are each individual ripples or tiny drops. When you can see that, being kind and loving and accepting others is not difficult. And when we behave toward others as we would like them to behave toward us, they then begin to behave like that toward us because we are all one.'

The monk pauses, then says reflectively, looking at Suzi, 'Maybe what I've just described is a good example for you of karma working.'

This brings back to me a very early memory from my childhood – my mother reading me *The Water Babies* by Charles

Kingsley. I couldn't bear the story because it made me feel too sad, but one thing in that book has always stayed with me and that's the example of "Mrs-do-as-you-would-be-done-by" whose message was to treat others as you want to be treated yourself. Honestly, why would we not?

The group is quiet. Maybe some of them, like me, are reflecting on aspects of their own childhood, wishing that they had had the kind of a start in life that the monk has been describing.

The monk smiles at us. 'That's quite a lot to absorb, he says. 'Are there any questions?'

There is something I have been wondering about, and thinking of Tina Turner earlier, and how helpful she found the Buddhist chanting brought it to my mind again. I hesitate. The monk catches my eye.

'Do you have a question, Rose?' he asks.

'Well, just a little thing', I say. 'Sometimes in the past I have used a mantra for meditating and I wondered what you think of that?'

The monk smiles and replies, 'A mantra – that is, a word or phrase that we repeat over and over as we meditate, silently or out loud – can be a helpful tool to use in meditation and we do use them sometimes in the Theravada tradition.

'We usually repeat the word "Buddho" (the same as the word in our chanting), which was the mantra that my teacher, Ajahn Sumedho recommended, particularly if our mind is very active. And he reminded us that when we say "Buddho" (which is pronounced like "good-doh" but with an initial 'B'), we are referring to what we call our own "Buddha nature", to the part within us that is pure and enlightened. We are calling on that, encouraging it to arise, not calling on the Buddha as a person.'

'We can combine the mantra, "Buddho", or whatever words we have chosen, with our breathing. We inhale as we say or think "Bud", and exhale on the "dho". This can be especially helpful in a walking meditation to help keep in sync with the rhythm of our movement.

'We use the energy of the mantra, "Buddho" to keep our mind clear and help put us in touch with our own clarity within – our own Buddha nature. So we do it with energy. "Bud", "Dho"', says the monk, in his powerful, melodious voice. 'Let's do a mantra meditation to conclude this session.'

We move a little, then settle ourselves. We are ready.

"Buddho" Meditation

'Gently take a few mindfulness breaths in and out, feeling the breath going in through your nostrils, then gently out again.

'After a few breaths, start to say "Bud" to yourself as you breathe in, and "Dho" as you breathe out.

'Let the breath, in or out, be at one with the sound. Feel that you are breathing the brightness of the word throughout your body. Keep breathing steadily...

'When you are ready, close by breathing some *metta* to yourself. Say "May I be well. May I be happy. May I be safe and free from harm."

'And then for all living beings say, "May all living beings be well. May they be happy. May they be safe and free from harm."'

There is a beautiful presence in the room. We sit for a few minutes more in silence, then we join in the closing chant as usual. We gently start to move and get up quietly to gather our things.

Quick Review

- The final group of qualities in the Eightfold Path are Right Effort, Right Mindfulness and Right Concentration.
- The Buddha said there are four aspects to Right Effort:
  - preventing negative states of mind, such as greed, hate and delusion from arising.
  - releasing those that have already arisen.
  - cultivating 'skilful' qualities, such as loving kindness, generosity and wisdom.
  - strengthening those 'skilful' qualities that we already have.
- Right Mindfulness means bringing our attention to the present moment. It is being aware of what we are experiencing right now in our surroundings, our body and our breathing. It is noticing, accepting and letting be without commenting, criticizing, judging, wishing or comparing.
- Right Concentration is about strengthening our resolve to put into practice the qualities of the Eightfold Path and keeping our mind and our intention focused on what we are doing.
- Intention, mindfulness and concentration are all it takes – plus a bit of effort. You can do it!

Practice

- Think about ways to support yourself in your practice. Organize your way of life to make it easier for you to follow the Eightfold Path.
- Be practical. Keep away from things that make it hard to follow the precepts. Be kind to yourself.
- Continue to make mindfulness part of your daily life whenever you think of it (or set your alarm). For example, you can be mindful when you're washing up, working at the computer or just walking along the pavement.
- Meditate each day for 20 minutes.
  - Continue with your *metta* practice at the end of your meditation, starting with yourself as usual, followed by a patron and then someone you love and finally someone you feel neutral about. Say to yourself: 'May I be safe. May I be happy. May I be well and at ease.' Picture your patron and say, 'May you be well. May you be happy. May you be safe and at ease'. Now visualize someone you love and say, 'May you be well. May you be happy. May you be safe and at ease'. Then imagine your neutral person and again say, 'May you be well. May you be happy. May you be safe and at ease.'

Week 8

Metta – Loving Kindness

*I*t's late July and our last meeting. The monk has arrived and people are assembling, chatting, laughing and taking their places. There's a feeling of expectancy, friendliness, warmth. I can't help contrasting this with the rather nervous, uncertain atmosphere at the beginning of our first session.

That was eight weeks ago, and in some ways it feels like another life to me now. And yet if you asked me how I've changed, I would find it hard to pinpoint anything in particular. I feel that I am calmer; I feel more relaxed, happier, more contented with things as they are.

I have found mindfulness practice really helpful, and it has become part of my life. I am sure that it has contributed to my state of mind. I am also finding I am becoming more and more aware of my feelings, such as impatience, irritation, nervousness, wanting and not wanting. I notice the feeling I'm experiencing and trace it back to the 'desire' that is behind it – one of the 'fearsome five', as I call them: greed, hate, delusion, clinging and craving.

And then I just accept that feeling. I can feel myself relax as I do so. And the tension, the 'charge' goes. It's amazing. It really does work. Accepting the feeling soothes it; it feels like putting a healing balm on a sore place.

I'm reflecting on this when I hear the monk's voice.

'Welcome and greetings', he is saying, 'it's so good to be with you all again'. He pauses, then adds with a twinkle, 'fellow travellers on the Eightfold Path.'

He laughs and we all join in.

For a ridiculous moment I see in my mind's eye a picture of the yellow brick road from *The Wizard of Oz* and hear the lyrics playing in my brain, 'Follow the yellow brick road, follow the yellow brick road. We're off to see the wizard, the wonderful wizard of Oz ...'

Goodness, what's the matter with me! Nice day-dream though. But the monk's voice breaks through my little reverie.

'So, does anyone have any questions? Any comments? Anything you'd like me to explain or clarify?' he asks. 'Anything at all you'd like to discuss or share with the group before we start?'

Pam puts up her hand and speaks. 'You did say before that if there was time you would say something else about reincarnation. I would like to know a little more about that.'

'Yes', replies the monk. 'Let's see ... When we get into the place of awareness within us where we can experience pure consciousness, we find that we are outside time in what the Dalai Lama describes as "an infinite dimension, without beginning and without end".

'If you accept this, then re-birth must occur to allow continuity of consciousness. We are here now, so we must have come from that consciousness and must return to it and possibly be reborn again – and again – perhaps numerous times. Or perhaps part of us never left that consciousness.

'I have seen examples of this when I was in one of the monasteries in Thailand, where reincarnation is widely accepted.

I have seen instances where a child who has died young has apparently been reborn quickly and has recognized possessions, places and relatives from their past life.

'Yes, Robert', the monk says, as Robert raises his hand. I know that reincarnation is a subject he has studied and it interests him very much.

'There was a particularly poignant example of reincarnation in a book I read', he says. 'It's an old one called *The Case for Reincarnation*. The author, Leslie Weatherhead, describes the experience that an Italian couple recounted to him.' He pauses.

'Would you like to tell us about it?' asks the monk.

'Yes. Apparently this Italian couple had a daughter called Blanche, and they employed a French-speaking Swiss nanny to look after her. The nanny used to sing a French lullaby to Blanche and she became very fond of it and asked for it to be sung repeatedly.

'Sadly, little Blanche died, the nanny left and the cradle song was forgotten and never heard in the house again.

'Then, three years later, Blanche's mother conceived another baby. When she was four months pregnant she had a strange waking dream in which Blanche appeared to her and said in her familiar voice, "Mother, I am coming back." Then the vision faded.

'The new baby girl was born. They called her Blanche, too, and she was said to closely resemble the first Blanche. When she was about six years old, an extraordinary thing happened. While her mother was sitting in the room next to Blanche's, she heard the distant sound of the famous cradle song that she had long forgotten.

'She went into Blanche's room and asked her who had taught her that song. "No one", replied the little girl. I just know it in my own head."

'And she continued to sing it joyfully as though she had never sung another song in her life. That's a true story, documented and signed.'

Although I've heard this story before – it's one of Robert's favourites – I feel shivers go down my spine when I hear it, as I always do. Everyone in the group is silent.

Then the monk says, 'Thank you, Robert, that was very interesting and moving.'

We are all silent for a while, then Pam speaks. 'I was once told by a medium I had been an Egyptian pharaoh queen – Nefertiti, in fact', she adds, pulling a face.

We all laugh, though I must admit, Pam does have an Egyptian look about her, apart from her blonde hair.

'Oh, there are quite a few Nefertitis around', says Suzi, laughing.

The monk pauses, smiles, then says, 'And doesn't our ego love to think we have been someone powerful, famous or exotic in a past life!'

Everyone laughs.

'As I said before,' he continues, 'I don't think it's advisable to dwell *too* much on past lives. It can be unhelpful because it can cause attachment to the concept of reincarnation, attachment to the past. And when you've touched the awareness of pure consciousness in meditation, details of individual past lives lose their importance.'

I catch the monk's eye.

'Is there something you'd like to say, Rose?' he asks.

I hesitate, but there is something I would like to know about. I decide to be brave and ask.

'Yes,' I say tentatively, 'it's something I've been wondering about since I've become interested in the Buddha's teaching. I was brought up to have a deep belief in angels, and I'd like to know the Buddhist view on this.'

The monk pauses and waits for a moment. *Oh no, I've said something wrong*, I think. Then he says, 'That sounds like an important belief for you.'

'Yes', I agree, 'but it's much more than a belief. My mother always said that she owed her life to the intervention of an angel.'

There is a rustling in the group, a feeling of expectation. I begin to wish I hadn't brought it up, but feel compelled to elaborate.

'It was when she was about ten years old', I begin, 'and my mother was living in the Australian bush at the time. She had the task of filling up the paraffin heater each morning, which I think was an extraordinary thing to ask a ten year-old to do, but that was her job. And one morning she was about to tip the liquid into the heater as usual, when she heard a voice inside her head say "Stop! Smell it first".

'She couldn't think why she heard that, but the power behind the voice was so great that she couldn't ignore it. She put her nose to the can and realized it didn't smell quite the same as usual, so she put it down and went to ask her father about it.

'It turned out that he had bought some petrol the day before and had got it put in the can that usually contained the paraffin for the stove. He praised my mother for her alertness and told her it had saved her life.

'She always said that it was an angel who had saved her and from that day on she was always aware of angels. She had several other experiences during the Second World War when she felt and saw them protecting her at times of extreme danger.

'So she passed on to me and my sister her complete trust in angels. I was rather a fearful little girl and I found it very comforting to know that I was protected by angels.

'I am still in touch with angels; they are an important part of my life', I continue, feeling rather embarrassed at pouring out so much personal information, and adding 'But now I am wondering what is the Buddhist approach to them?'

'Thank you for sharing that moving experience', replies the monk, thoughtfully. 'Buddhist teaching does embrace angels. We call them *devas*, and they are mentioned in many of the Buddha's discourses. In fact, the Buddha was described as "a teacher of *devas* and humans".

'As we have said before, the Buddha's teaching is experiential. He asks you only to take from it what feels right and true for you.

Take what is helpful. If none of it is helpful, then leave it alone. There is no pressure.

'Some of you may well not accept the presence or intervention of angels. That is fine. Rose, you on the other hand have had experiences that have shown you the existence and presence of angels in your life, and they have proved helpful. That is fine, too.'

'Yes, but what about delusion?' asks Tim. 'In the Second Noble Truth we are warned by the Buddha about being attached to delusion. For me, angels would come into this category.'

'Follow what resonates with you, Tim. Remember the words of the Buddha that I mentioned earlier and only accept what "agrees with your own reason and common sense".'

'Does that mean we can adopt a "pick-and-mix" approach to Buddhism, going along with the bits we like?' Tim asks.

The monk pauses before replying, then says, 'As I said at the very beginning of this course, everything you need in order to follow the Buddhist path and live a happy, free and peaceful life is contained within the Four Noble Truths. They include Right View – being aware of what is going on within your body, mind and emotions; mindfulness; *metta* and finding that place of peace, awareness and wisdom within your own being. And also the Eightfold Path, which is of course the Fourth Noble Truth.

'There is a tendency for people to take on board the first three Noble Truths – or parts of them. For example, "mindfulness" and "being in the now" have become modern catchphrases and now form part of many therapies. But they neglect or overlook the rest, particularly the Fourth Noble Truth, which includes a code of ethics.

'Some people do not like the idea of a code of ethics, but practising the Fourth Noble Truth is just as essential to your happiness, freedom from suffering and peace, as the first three Noble Truths are.

'Without the code of ethics you will only get so far, because those rules – no lying, no stealing, no sexual abuse, no taking of life, no abuse of intoxicants – are designed to help you to live in a way that creates conditions of happiness, freedom and peace within you and in the world.

'Belief in angels is optional – although acceptance of a spirit world and of angels and the supernatural does make up part of Right View, according to the Buddha, but following the code of ethics outlined in the Eightfold Path and expressed in the Five Precepts, is a requirement. We need it to keep ourselves clean and clear, so that we feel a sense of congruence throughout our being.'

'As you practise the first three Noble Truths, you may find that you are automatically putting into practice the Fourth Noble Truth, including the five precepts, without thinking about it. It follows on naturally and they are all interlinked, as we've noticed before. But if you do it purposefully, it will speed up your progress in the inner work – if we can use the word "progress" for once.'

The monk reflects for a moment and smiles. 'People sometimes think that the Buddhist way is serious and rather solemn, but that is not the case. The Buddha was full of fun and humour. He said, if you remember, "There is no path to happiness, happiness *is* the path."

'It's a path of joy and happiness! Be happy. Be at peace. Be full of joy. That's the way of the Buddha – happiness, peace and joy for all people, all living creatures; we are all one. And remember, it begins with *you*.'

Gwyn puts up her hand.

'Yes?' asks the monk.

Gwyn pauses. 'Does that include animals? Are they part of the "oneness"?'

'Just as the Buddha discouraged questions about an individual permanent soul, he also discouraged speculation about this', replies the monk.

There is a pause, then he adds reflectively, almost as an afterthought: 'In Zen Buddhist teaching there is the expression, "All is one and all is different." There is a *koan* – a riddle – that goes, "What is the difference between the enlightened and the unenlightened person?"

'Do any of you know the answer to that?' he asks, smiling.

'You're joking', replies Rodney.

But the monk is serious. He continues, 'The answer is that the unenlightened person sees a difference, but the enlightened person does not. But, where has this got us?'

'Confused', replies Pam, and laughs.

'Quite so, quite so', replies the monk. 'You see why the Buddha discouraged such discussions?'

'Oh, I'm sorry' says Gwyn, quietly, her composure disturbed for a moment.

'No, it's fine', says the monk. 'I did not mean that we need to avoid such a deep and interesting question. Please continue.'

Gwyn smiles shyly, and says, 'It's just that when I'm in my garden or when I'm meditating, feeling love and peace in my heart, I feel as if I'm connected with every living thing. It seems as though there are golden threads of light connecting everything – the birds, the bees, the animals, the insects ... even the trees and plants. It's a feeling of such peace and joy, I can't really put it into words. That's why I asked.'

The monk looks at her kindly, and smiles. 'I think you can trust your experience', he replies, then adds, almost as an afterthought, 'and you certainly have Mahatma Gandhi on your side. He said, "My ethics not only permit me to claim but require me to *own* kinship with not merely the ape but the horse and the sheep, the lion and the leopard, the snake and the scorpion."'

'Was Gandhi a Buddhist?' asks Rodney, after a pause.

'He considered that he was', says the monk. 'He said that Buddhism was rooted in Hinduism and represented its purest essence. But I think we're getting a bit off-topic again.'

Maurice catches the monk's eye.

'You've spoken about "enlightenment" a lot', he says, 'but I'm not really clear what exactly that means.'

'That makes two of us', jokes the monk, laughing, 'but you'll know it when you achieve it, they say.

'To be a bit more serious', he adds, 'it is usually defined as freedom from what the Buddha called *dukka* or suffering. It's the full realization of the truth of the Buddha's teaching.

'It has nothing to do with intellect, supernatural states or spiritual visions. Enlightenment in the Buddhist sense is not concerned with knowledge or intellect, either. Enlightenment is here,' he says, putting his hand on his heart, 'not here', pointing to his forehead.

'It is being in that awakened state of awareness, clarity and luminescence that we learned of in the Third Noble Truth. It's the state of purity that we were born with before we built the structure of our ego and we can find it again; anyone can – and they can do it in this life. Ajahn Sumedho, my teacher, was very clear about this. Enlightenment is not beyond the reach of anyone in this life. Anyone and everyone can find it by following and practising the Four Noble Truths.'

The monk pauses. '... Which brings us back to where we started at the beginning of the course.

The monk looks around the group.

'So, he says. 'Now I am going to tell you a true story. It's about 'metta' – loving kindness.'

We move around, settle and wait for the monk to speak.

'One day' he says, 'at the time of the Buddha, a group of his monks went into the forest to meditate. They set off cheerfully and happily, but when they got deeper in among the dark trees, they became very alarmed by strange noises, which they thought came from evil spirits. So, full of fear, they fled back to the Buddha.

'He responded by taking them through a *metta* process, in which they sent out loving kindness toward the evil spirits. Then, he sent them back into the forest to get on with their meditating. It must have worked because after that they stayed in the forest for a long time, so the story goes.

'As you have found during this course, we don't need to be in a forest and beset by strange noises and "evil spirits" to benefit from *metta*. I have explained before that sending *metta* to ourselves and others is a simple and helpful technique that we can do in any place at any time, and if you do it regularly, it can change your life. In fact, it's one of the fastest ways to bring about change.

'I go so far as to say if you only take *one thing* away with you from this course, make it the practice of *metta* – "Dr Buddha's" best all-purpose medicine! If you want a living example of the power of *metta*, you don't have to look any further than the Dalai Lama, who says, "My religion is loving kindness".'

The monk pauses, then he adds, 'Now that is a serious statement, not a flippant comment. It's something to really ponder, something to think about. The more you practise *metta* yourself, the more you'll understand just how profound those words of the Dalai Lama really are.'

He stops for a moment, then says very quietly, almost to himself, 'I do sometimes wonder what life would be like if everyone in the world followed the religion of loving kindness.'

We're all quiet. Through the French windows I notice the shadows in the garden beginning to lengthen. There is such a peaceful, loving atmosphere in the group. For a moment my mind wanders, then I come back to the monk's voice.

'Metta – loving kindness – is a wonderful antidote to fear, anger, hate, jealousy, sadness, uncertainty, worry – you name it! And you can't overdose on it. The more you practise loving kindness in your life, the better the result and the better you'll feel.

'The Buddha told his followers that the practice of *metta* had many benefits. Here are some of them: "Sleeping easily, waking easily, dreaming no evil dreams"; being "dear to human beings, dear to non-human beings"; being "protected by *devas*" and protected from "fire, poison and weapons"; having good concentration and a "bright complexion"; dying "unconfused and heading for the *Brahma* world (heaven) and "good birth" in their next incarnation.

'We have to remember that when the Buddha was teaching, many of his followers were Hindus who had deep beliefs in reincarnation, so they were particularly interested in following a practice that would ensure they would be reborn next time into good conditions.

'The Buddha added, however, that whatever were the merits of practising *metta* to ensure a "good birth", they did not reach even one sixteenth of those brought about by the "liberation of mind" that the practice of *metta* brings and "shines forth, bright and brilliant".'

In the pause that follows, Sam looks at the monk, catches his eye then looks down.

'Do you have a question, Sam?' asks the monk, kindly.

'Yes,' replies Sam rather hesitantly. 'That all sounds very good and I've been trying my best with the *metta* practice throughout the course, but the trouble is – I don't know how to put this ... ' he hesitates, then continues haltingly, 'but I find it very difficult to feel anything in my heart – love, or anything. I mean, I've been doing the *metta* practice you told us about and I try to be a decent person, but where emotion is concerned I feel kind of ... numb.'

'That is not uncommon', says the monk gently, 'and I must reassure you that it doesn't mean that you don't have a loving heart. We all do; it is part of being alive. We all start with easy access to our core of love and kindness, but as we grow up and experience the hurts and disappointments of life, we protect ourselves by putting barriers around that sensitive, inner part of us, by building our ego-house around ourselves.

'So when we try to contact the love that is within us, we can feel closed off from our emotions. Our heart may feel numb. We know we do love others and we want to feel it, but we can't.

'For many of us this protective shell, this ego-house around our heart, gets broken when we fall in love and we touch our inner core of love and kindness – the feeling of openness, of being at one with another person.'

There is silence in the group again. Maybe others are remembering, as I am, the thrill and rapture of being in love:

that giddy, heady, euphoria when our senses are heightened and everything feels magical, more colourful, more beautiful, than ever before.

I'm having a bit of a reverie when the monk continues, 'But of course, this doesn't last.' He pauses for a moment, then adds, 'However, the good news is that through practising *metta* – and indeed all of the techniques we have shared during our time together – we can reconnect with that inner core of loving kindness and experience that joy and rapture that feels like being in love.

The monk pauses again, then says, 'When you get the hang of *metta*, it's like being in love with the whole world, feeling *rapture* all the time.'

'Did you know', the monk adds, 'that the Buddha said, "Rapture is the gateway to *nirvana*"?'

I don't think any of us did know that. I certainly didn't. In fact, before I started this course, as I've said before, I really did think that Buddhism was all about suffering, denying oneself, being quite prim and proper, rather po-faced, pursed-lipped and disapproving of any kind of excess or celebration.

Now the monk is telling us – from the Buddha himself, no less – that being happy or rapturous – is in fact the 'gateway to *nirvana*'. And, not only that, but you have to start by loving yourself. I'm quite thunderstruck.

'But to return to the question', continues the monk, 'We can get back that rapture, get back that loving feeling'.

For a moment I can't help hearing the sound of the Righteous Brothers singing, "You've lost that lovin' feeling", playing in my head. I think: *Pull yourself together. You're getting a bit light-headed with all this talk of being in love'.* I try to focus on the monk's words.

'We can get back in touch with that love and openness, that rapture even, with regular *metta* practice. We may have to go through the process at first without feeling much, but the miracle is that if we do it regularly, gradually the blocks and barriers around our heart – the blocks and barriers of our ego-house that stop us feeling – begin to melt.

'To put it another way and mix my metaphors a bit, if you'll excuse me, our heart is like a tight rosebud gradually opening within us as the sun, in the form of *metta*, shines on it. The practice of loving kindness really can transform us. We shine the warm sun of *metta* on our tight, numb heart and it opens.'

The monk pauses to collect his thoughts. He looks directly at Sam and then around the group. 'Trust me, trust the wisdom of the Buddha', he says. 'Trust the experience of thousands and thousands of the Buddha's followers down the ages – over two millennia. It works, it truly *works*.

'It may well feel unnatural at first, like any new skill, for we're exercising the "heart muscle" that hasn't been used for a while. It may feel a bit as though you are having to "fake it before you make it" to begin with. But little by little you'll get it running again, connect with it and – this I promise you – it will transform your life, and the lives of all those around you. Just *do* it.

'The process of opening the heart begins like this. Love yourself. Be kind to yourself. Concentrate on the feeling you get inside you when you think of someone or something that you know you love – perhaps a beloved pet. Cultivate that warm feeling, and it will grow and widen. Watch your self-talk – that critical, harsh inner voice, we mentioned earlier. Speak kindly to yourself as if you were a beloved child. Cherish your own inner child, as they say.

'You have to get that inner child feeling loved, happy, healthy and full of joy first, before you can truly love others. I liken it to the announcement they make on aircraft about making sure your own oxygen mask is in place before helping others fit theirs.

'It always seems so selfish to indulge oneself', says Pam. 'I find it really difficult.'

'Yes, many of us do,' agrees the monk.

'But you cannot give loving kindness to others until you have connected with that well of loving kindness within yourself. Then, once you have become comfortable with being kind to yourself, you will find it a lot easier – natural, in fact – to start extending it into your life. You can give *metta* to your partner, children, family and friends, your pets, the people who have helped you in your life, your neighbours, even people you don't have any particular feelings for. And then – wait for it – extend *metta* to the people you find difficult, challenging, really dislike or even hate and despise.'

The monk stops. There is a movement in the group, some murmurs of surprise.

'People we actually *hate*? People we despise, such as mass murderers, for example?' asks Suzi, incredulously.

'Yes', replies the monk, firmly.

'Well really!' exclaims Rodney. 'That's a bit much. I don't think I could ever do that. I couldn't forgive Hitler, for instance, let alone feel love and compassion for him. Where's the justice in that?'

'What justice?' asks the monk. 'Excluding people you hate and despise from your practice of loving kindness brings "justice", does it?'

There is a pause, then the monk says thoughtfully, 'Do you think that bringing people like Hitler to "justice" for something they have done in the past helps anyone?'

'Yes, it sets an example to others', says Rodney.

'So is "setting others a good example" a valid reason for punishing someone, do you think?' asks the monk.

'That sounds to me a bit like making them into a scapegoat', comments Tim.

'Yes', replies the monk, 'and we need to be careful that we are not punishing the offender out of vengeance or to seek revenge. If we do that, we become mixed up in the karma and it all gets very complicated and messy.'

'But isn't punishment karma for doing wrong?' asks Suzi.

The monk thinks, then adds, 'Perhaps. According to the Buddha, evil actions certainly create karma. But I think we can trust the

Law of Karma to work perfectly well without our assistance.'

'So we have to go soft on crime, then, do we?' asks Rodney. 'We may be Buddhist, but we have to be realistic.'

We are all silent; Rodney is stony-faced.

'Could you tell me, Rodney', asks the monk, 'how your heart feels at this moment when you are thinking of Hitler and the need for "justice"?'

I feel sorry for Rodney being put on the spot like this, but the monk is looking at him kindly, radiating warmth and love himself.

There is a long pause, then Rodney says, rather quietly, 'I can't feel anything.'

After another pause he adds 'I feel disconnected from my heart at the moment. It just feels hard. I can't feel any love. I'm just thinking of all those millions of people who perished as a result of Hitler's actions.'

'So', says the monk, 'hard rocks of hurt, anger and the desire for revenge are sitting there in your heart, blocking the flow of the stream of love that is your true and natural state. What good are those hard rocks doing to anyone? To the people who perished? To you? To the world? You are certainly not punishing Hitler, you are punishing yourself.

'Being "realistic", as you said before, means accepting the situation here and now, exactly as it is; feeling the suffering inside you – all that rage and hurt toward Hitler and all the millions of people who suffered. Feel it; really, really feel it –

your feelings about it, *your* feelings towards Hitler. Just feel them without comment and let them be. And, if you keep doing this, what will happen?'

The monk stops. We are all silent.

'You will find that they go. All that hurt and rage will diminish. Those rocks that are blocking your heart and hurting you will melt like ice in the sun. "Letting it be" will become "letting go", and then you'll be free.

'And in the process, in time, you'll touch that clarity and awareness that lies right at your core and find there's no person there – no "me", no "Hitler" and no one else either. There's no need for judgment, no need for revenge; just perfect peace and love and kindness. Because when we get beneath all the hard, protective layers of the ego and dissolve the stones and bricks, that's all there is.'

Once again, the monk's words have brought a tangible feeling of love and peace – bliss, even – into the room. I breathe it in. I feel so happy. Then I hear his voice continuing.

'Now, practising the Four Noble Truths in our life can help us get there. All we need for a happy life and to reach nirvana can be written on a postcard, remember? When in doubt, always go back to the Four Noble Truths. They will never let you down.

'But alongside that you can practise *metta*. That gets you there, too, if you do it really diligently. That supports and nurtures your work on the Four Noble Truths, supercharges your car, speeds up your journey, as it were.

'You see, when we truly love ourselves through our *metta* practice, we begin to get in touch with our own humanity – our pain, our sadness, our dashed hopes, our fears. We attend to these and we begin to see them in other people, too.

'We realize that other people are just like us – they want happiness; they want safety; they want security; they want to be respected, valued, loved. Why would they not? Tell me', the monk repeats slowly, '*Why would they not?*'

'When we think like this, we get to the point where we feel open and loving and accepting of everyone. We see the neediness, the hopes, the dashed expectations and the hurt in others. We feel as if these are all our own.

'It gets to the point where we begin to feel this with everyone we meet, everyone we hear about on the news. We just become open to them, at one with them. That's what *metta* does.

'We see that all living beings – including, for the record, animals – want love and understanding. They want kindness, they want happiness – just like we do. All of us. We just can't do anything to harm any of them. It feels like harming ourselves.

That's the same as the precepts in the Eightfold Path – not to take life, not to steal, not to abuse others sexually, not to lie – you get to the point where you can't do anything hurtful or unkind to others because it feels – it really and truly feels, sometimes even physically – as though you are doing it to yourself, hurting yourself. Which of course you are, from a karmic point of view.' the monk adds thoughtfully.

He continues, 'A really useful rule of thumb is to t
including animals – as you yourself would like to be treated. It s
not rocket science, you know.

'So, after all that, let's remember the story I told you about
the Buddha and his monks and their *metta* meditation, and go
through the full *metta* practice that the Buddha gave, which is
still used today in Buddhist monasteries all over the world.

'It is a specific process of directing *metta* – loving kindness –
to five different people. We start with ourselves, as we've been
doing during this course. Then we take four other people in turn,
picturing each one and thinking – or, if you can, feeling – *metta*
toward them.

'The first is someone who has been kind and helpful to us –
someone who the Buddha would have described as a patron or
benefactor. It could be a parent, a teacher, a boss or a neighbour.
The next person we imagine is someone we like very much or
love, perhaps our partner or child. Then we conjure up someone
we feel neutral about, for example, someone who has served us in
our local shop; and finally, we visualize someone we find difficult,
someone we dislike, despise or even hate.

'You could practise sending *metta* to Hitler', the monk says,
looking at Rodney. 'It doesn't matter that he's dead; you're
sending *metta* to the Hitler in your heart. Do you remember
the story I told you before about the monk who carried the
beautiful woman over the river? And his companion, the monk
who was so disgusted he continued to carry the woman in his

mind long afterward? Are you still carrying Hitler in your heart?

'Send *metta* to that part of you. When you can do that, you'll know that you truly understand the practice of *metta* – and you will experience amazing lightness of being. The space you make in your heart by dissolving the bitterness and anger – your inner Hitler – will fill with love, kindness and happiness.

'When we do a *metta* meditation, we do our best to send *metta* to each of those four people in turn – five, including ourselves. Even if we can't feel the feeling, we can say the words to ourselves.

'You can even go on a "*metta* intensive", taking each category in turn, starting with yourself, and spend several days or even a week or more just concentrating on sending *metta* to them, until you've completed all four other people.

'That's what we sometimes do in the monastery. Then, after the monks have been practising *metta* meditation all day long for several weeks...' continues the monk,

'*All day long for several weeks?* ...' interjects Suzi with a gasp.

The monk nods and smiles, 'Yes, after they have been practising *metta* meditation all day for several weeks, one of the questions they are asked is this.

"Imagine you are in the forest with your benefactor – the person who has been kind and helpful to you – and your loved one, your neutral person and someone you hate – your enemy. (Maybe that would be Hitler, for you, Rodney.) And you meet a group of bandits who demand that you choose one person in your group to be sacrificed. Who would you pick to die?'

The monk pauses. 'Think about it. Which one of you would it be?

There is a long silence. No one can answer.

'Maybe I need to wait until you've all practised the full *metta* meditation diligently for a while, then ask you again', comments the monk. 'I think if I did, the answer you would give might be different then.'

'But now let's do our *metta* practice. Today we are going to put it all together and follow the practice that the Buddha gave to his monks. Remember, this is a specific process of directing loving kindness to five different people, as I described before.

'If you are ready, let us begin our *metta* meditation.'

Metta Meditation

'Sit comfortably with your spine straight, holding it a little away from the back of your chair if you can manage it.

'Take your awareness to your breathing. Notice the breath going in and out: in through your nostrils, down into your lungs and then out again through your nostrils.

Now bring your attention to the centre of your chest, to your heart centre.

'To get your 'metta muscle' working, think of something or someone that makes you feel loved. It might be a lover, past or present; it might be a little child, a beloved parent, a precious pet. It doesn't matter who or what, it's whatever or whoever arouses the feeling of love in you.

'Feel that love and kindness; feel the warm glow in your heart. This will get easier with practice. If you find it difficult to feel, then imagine the feeling instead.

'Stay with this feeling of love for a few moments. Breathe in and out steadily. Enjoy the feeling of warmth and love, like a golden sun, in the centre of your being.

'Feel that love and kindness. Love and kindness are our natural state; we all have love and kindness at our core.

'As you breathe in, direct the love and kindness to yourself. If you can, visualize the light within your heart expanding to surround your whole body, like being wrapped in warm sunshine. Then say these metta words to yourself: "May I be safe. May I be happy. May I be well and at ease."'

'Now think of someone who has helped you – your "patron" – as the Buddha called them. Visualize them in your mind; feel the loving kindness flowing from your heart to them. You may feel a warm, golden glow in your heart, like the sun, and see this ever expanding so that it bathes them in golden light. Then say "May you be safe. May you be happy. May you be well and at ease."

'Next, think of someone you love; visualize them, feel the golden glow in your heart and your love going out to them. See them bathed in golden light, and say, "May you be safe. May you be happy. May you be well and at ease."

'Now, think of someone you feel neutral about, someone you have no strong feelings for either way. Repeat the process with the love and the golden light; and say, "May you be safe. May you be happy. May you be well and at ease."

'Next, think of someone you have difficulty with or whom you dislike or even hate and go through the same process. Think *metta* to them even if you can't feel it, but if you can send love to them, do so. If you can feel the warm glow of your heart, like a sun, expand and enfold them, do so, and say, "May you be safe. May you be happy. May you be be well and at ease."

'Feel this love in your heart. Feel it expand to everyone in this room, everyone in this village, this county, this country, this world ... outward and outward and still more outward.

'Even if you can't feel the love or see the golden light, go through the motions. Little by little your heart will wake up; the rosebud will open; the love you are getting back in touch with will start to rise up and melt those blocks of ego ice.

'As you do this more and more, and go deeper into the practice, you will find that the boundaries around you melt away. You are without boundary, you are part of everyone and every thing: the sky, the trees, the mountains, the rivers, the seas, the people, the birds, the mammals, the reptiles, the insects. You are one with the whole universe.

'Let us open our hearts in gratitude for this experience, for the time we have had together today and throughout this course. Breathe in, let your heart expand and fill with gratitude.

'Now come back gently to your surroundings. Take a few slow breaths and gently open your eyes.

I enjoy the meditation. Sending *metta* to people feels like a really positive thing to do and makes me feel good.

People begin to move gently. There is a tangible feeling of peace, of bliss, in the room. Such a simple process, yet so profound.

The monk looks round the group kindly, and smiles. 'Well, how was that?' he asks. 'You can practise it formally, as we have just done, or you can do it whenever you think about it throughout the day, in any spare moment – and certainly when you feel stressed, anxious, angry or worried. You can take one person from the group each day or each week, and work on them, always starting each practice period with yourself, of course.

'I have found that when I have had a disagreement or an "upset" with someone, it takes about a fortnight of daily *metta* practice, sending loving kindness to them as we have done just now, to resolve and release the issue in my heart. And what a feeling of peace that brings!

'The more you do this meditation, the easier and more natural it will become. You really will find that your capacity for loving kindness grows, your heart expands and, eventually, you will feel at one with every living being.

'I can't imagine ever feeling like that', says Rodney.

There is a pause. The monk looks at Rodney, then says, 'You know there is a saying by Henry Ford, something you may well have heard but I think it bears repeating. He said, "There are two types of people in the world: those who think they can and those who think they can't.'"

The monk pauses, then says, 'And they're both right'.

After a moment, we all 'get' it and there is general laughter.

'As the Buddha said', continues the monk, '"Our thoughts are the forerunners of our action". Of course, you can do it. Make the intention to get there – but don't be attached to it,' he adds with a laugh.

'Make space in your heart and your mind to allow it to happen – and it will. These practices work, if you work at them. One step at a time – and just keep on stepping.

There is a pause, then Gwyn says quietly, 'Being the motherly type – or maybe I should say "grandmotherly..."

Now, there's a surprise. I look at her slender frame and immaculate appearance and think she looks as though she'd be more at home on a catwalk than in a nursery. It just goes to show how misleading it can be to judge by appearances.

But Gwyn is continuing '... I find it helpful to think of the difficult person as a vulnerable small child who is misunderstood, sad or suffering. In my mind's eye, I look at their face and I find it really easy to hug or cuddle them, and "make it all better" for them by loving them, as one does with one's own children.

'It's the same with animals. I look into their little faces, see the hurt, the misunderstanding, the suffering and I just want to hug them, make them better, give them love, take their pain away.'

'Thank you for sharing that,' says the monk. 'That is a lovely way of looking at things, Gwyn. I think you've truly found *metta*.'

The monk stops for a moment, thinking, then says, looking directly at Gwyn, 'Just to ask you a quick question, if I may?'

Gwyn nods, and the monk continues, 'Coming back to the story of the bandits and the five people: yourself; someone who has been kind and helpful to you; your loved one; your neutral person; and someone you hate or find difficult, can you tell me now, Gwyn, which of those five people you would sacrifice to the bandits?'

There is silence. Gwyn looks down. We're all waiting for her answer – each of us glad, perhaps, that we're not the one being asked.

'I'm afraid I can't answer that', says Gwyn finally after a long pause, 'because I can't choose between them.'

'You wouldn't choose yourself then, because self-love is so important?' asks the monk.

There is another long pause. I feel really sorry for Gwyn being put on the spot like this, but after a while she replies, quite calmly, 'No. I'm sorry. It's weird, but I just can't seem to differentiate between myself and any of the others. We all seem to be one; I love us all equally. So I'm so sorry, I can't answer your question.'

Gwyn looks sad. There is another pause, then the monk smiles broadly and says, 'Thank you, Gwyn. You just have. That is the correct answer.

Gwyn begins to smile and laughs a little, then we follow. The monk continues: 'You see, when you really "get" *metta*, you realize we're all one.

'You will know you've "got" *metta* when you can let someone else be exactly as they are, even if you disapprove of them – or they disapprove of you – and love them just the same; when you feel open-hearted and accepting of everyone; when you can hear their good news and celebrate their success and joy exactly as if it were your own. And that is the most joyful feeling imaginable.

'You can measure your "degree of *metta*" by these simple tests without, let us hope, having to go into the forest and face a group of bandits!

'And now, you know, I think we've reached our destination – for the time being, at any rate. Now let us finish with a little chant, our closing homage to the Buddha.'

The monk takes a breath and his melodious voice fills the room once more. The group is joining in as usual from their chanting sheets. The words float out, then gently die away.

The monk bows his head slightly, puts his hands together in the prayer position and touches them to his head and then his heart. He pauses with his eyes closed.

We respond by bowing our heads and putting our hands to our hearts. There is a beautiful feeling of peace and gratitude as we sit in silence for a minute or two. Then the monk looks up and smiles.

The group moves gently and people start to gather their things, talking a little among themselves, picking up meditation mats, blankets and cushions. They find their shoes, collect their bags and leave the shrine room.

I open the front door and the cool early-evening air blows into the hall. People are hugging, saying 'Thank you'. There is laughter and joy – plenty of *metta*. Some of the men are kindly helping Robert to move sofas and tables back into position.

When they have all gone, there is just the monk, Robert and me remaining. I say 'Thank you so very much. That was life-changing; I can't thank you enough.'

The monk smiles: 'I am so glad', he says, simply. He takes his bowl and walks to the car with Robert, who is going to drive him back to the monastery.

I'm standing in the doorway. I put my hands together in the prayer position and bow my head slightly again. The car pulls out of the driveway and turns into the road.

I walk slowly back into the house and into the sitting room. The sofas are back in place but the altar still remains, with the Buddha and the flowers. The presence of the day, the peace and joy, linger – it is almost tangible. I sit for a moment in front of the altar and breathe it in.

It was a good course.

Quick Review

- Practising the Four Noble Truths, including *metta* and mindfulness, lead to happiness, freedom and peace. That is the way of the Buddha who said: "There is no path to happiness; happiness *is* the path."
- 'Enlightenment' means freedom from suffering, the full realization of the truth of the Buddha's teaching. It is being in an awakened state of bliss, awareness, clarity, luminescence and union with all living beings and is something anyone can realize for themselves by following the Four Noble Truths.
- *Metta* is a wonderful antidote to fear, anger, hate, jealousy, sadness, uncertainty, worry – any negative state. You can't overdose on it. The more you practise loving kindness, the more *metta* you feel.
- All we need for a happy life and 'to reach nirvana' can be written on a postcard. When in doubt, always go back to the Four Noble Truths, as they will never let you down.

Final Words

- Continue with your mindfulness practice. Have 'mindfulness minutes' throughout the day whenever you can; make mindfulness a way of life.
- Meditate every day for 20 to 30 minutes.
- Include *metta* practice at the end or the beginning of your

meditation often, and always if you are in pain or have issues with people. It is the fastest route to pain-relief and healing, whether physical, emotional or mental.

- Do walking meditations and body scan meditations often.
- Enjoy and be grateful for the happiness, freedom and peace you will experience.

Epilogue

What Happened Next

*I*t's more than a year now since that day when I opened my door to the monk and participated in the course that has, without doubt, changed my life. I went into it with no expectations for myself. As far as I was concerned, I was simply facilitating it and I attended it for the sake of my husband Robert.

The fact that it made such an impact on me and had far-reaching effects in my life, was due in no small part to the monk himself. He was such a shining example of his teaching: wise, humorous, kind, down-to-earth, radiant and happy. Spiritual or religious leaders can preach all they like, but it's how they speak and how they act – especially how much *metta* they radiate – that demonstrates the quality of their teaching.

Then there were a couple of things that the monk said quite early on, which really grabbed my attention and made me sit up and take notice.

The first was that Buddhism gives you everything you need for living a life of happiness, freedom and peace, and *that it is so simple you can write it on the back of a postcard.* I really loved that idea – I still do – and, indeed, I am finding it to be true.

The second thing was when, again early on, in one of the meditations, the monk told us to let go of 'becoming', of striving after goals in our life and to let things be, and see what would happen. He told us to bring our attention to the present, to notice the feeling we have 'of stress, of wanting, or not wanting, of trying to make things different from the way they are', and to allow everything simply to be the way it is.

And then he asked us what we thought would happen if we did that, and he challenged us to try it for ourselves and see.

This really intrigued me. The monk was so firm, so certain. I thought at the time that he meant that by letting go, by stopping trying to make things happen and practising the mindfulness meditation, I would change my life and create in it all the things I wanted. And of those there were many, I can assure you. I still have the lists and vision boards (collages made up of pictures of all the things we want to create in our life) to prove it.

Gradually, as I tried to put into practice the Buddha's teaching, I found I became calmer, more relaxed, more peaceful and more harmonious both within myself and with life in general. I think a great deal of this was due to the fact that I was – and still am – noticing my thoughts more and taking mindfulness breaths as often as I remember – I really like the 'mindfulness minute' and the 'short-time, many-times' approach to meditation that the monk taught us.

Another thing that made a huge difference to me – and I know I've mentioned this before but I just can't believe the positive effect this has had – is stopping judging, comparing, criticizing and condemning. We are so used to doing this – being witty or funny at the expense of others; making ourselves feel superior by criticizing someone or comparing ourselves to other people and feeling inferior ourselves because someone else is better looking, cleverer, more successful, richer and so on – that to stop comparing and criticizing seems so unnatural at first.

To start with, when I made an effort to stop judging, comparing, criticizing and condemning, I did not know how to reply when someone else criticized or condemned someone or something, but all that has fallen into place now as I have found some new conversation strategies. One of these I've borrowed straight from that wise and wonderful monk, Ajahn Chah, who would frequently respond to judgments, comparisons, criticism and condemnation with the words, 'Is that so'.

I also notice that I'm often saying, 'Oh well, it is as it is' and another Ajahn Chah-ism that I find helpful is 'good enough'. 'It's good enough'; 'She or he is good enough'; and, most of all, 'I'm good enough'.

There's no doubt that I have certainly become happier and more comfortable within myself. I can't tell you what a great feeling it is to put on the television or read a newspaper and not automatically start criticizing everything and everyone. For example, making comments such as, 'What *does* she think she looks like?' or 'Goodness, what an idiot!' or 'How stupid!' or 'How greedy!' and so on.

Now, from my own experience, I realize that thinking those thoughts and making those comments makes *me* feel uncomfortable and destroys *my* own inner peace. It's so much more comfortable to be able to view life 'as it is', without criticism.

It's all part of accepting things in this present moment, as they are. 'It is as it is', as the monk said. I had heard this before, but I had never really taken it to heart. But now it is so obvious;

accepting things – situations and people – exactly as they are brings extraordinary peace.

Something else that I have found helpful has been consciously taking the decision not to be offended. Taking offence does absolutely no good, it just continues the pain – and it's often based on assumption and misunderstanding anyway. But once I started looking out for this, I was surprised how often I found I was on the verge of doing it – and stopped myself in time.

One of the things I've realized is that when you take offence or hold on to hurts and grudges, when you condemn and criticize others, you are only hurting yourself; you are taking your anger toward the offence or the person who committed it out on yourself.

So with practice, acceptance has now become so natural to me that I find when I think or say something critical or judgmental, I get a physical pain in my heart. I've exchanged the fun of occasional gossip and 'setting the world to rights' with a feeling of inner peace and joy. Not a bad swap.

In some ways, though, it's difficult to be the judge of one's own changes, because many of them just seem to happen gradually and naturally. Sometimes it's other people who notice them, especially when you haven't seen them for a while.

This was brought home to me some time after the course when I visited my daughter, son-in-law and baby grandson, whom I had not seen for several months. It was a small thing, but very telling.

We had spent a sunny morning at the seaside near where they live. We enjoyed it so much that time passed quickly and it was getting rather late for the coffee we'd planned to have at a very lovely and popular café at the other end of the beach.

My daughter asked 'Shall we go for coffee? It will be crowded at this time, so we'll probably have to queue.'

'Oh, yes, let's go', I replied. 'If we have to queue, we have to queue.'

There was a stunned, shocked silence. My daughter looked at me in amazement. I didn't know what was the matter with her. Then she said 'Mum! That's not like you!

Where's that woman who, when I was with her in Goa, had to get up at 5am to make sure she had a lounger in a place where no one could lie in front and block her view? You have changed!'

I don't think I really want to share the lounger episode and I'm not certain I wouldn't have another lapse if the situation arose again, but there's no doubt that I really am feeling so much calmer, more at peace, centred, loving and happier in myself than I ever have before. That is something for which I am truly and forever thankful.

And the way things have turned out recently, I've needed it, I can tell you. Not long after the course, Robert drove out in his car one evening. I was expecting him back home by about 8.00pm at the latest and when it got to after 9pm and there was no sign of him and no message from him, it was hard not to fear the worst. I phoned the police and there had been no reports of road accidents, so I just had to wait. I could not understand why he didn't phone me.

Eventually, well after 10pm, a breakdown lorry arrived at our gateway with Robert in the front and his car on the back. He had filled the tank with petrol instead of diesel, so the car had seized up after a few miles. The shock had been so great that he had completely lost his memory – which was why he hadn't phoned.

He had managed to get home thanks to the kindness of strangers, but he was completely helpless. He couldn't remember where he lived, didn't recognize our house or me; he was a different person.

Over the following weeks his memory did return a little. He had tests and scans and was found to be suffering from Lewy Body Dementia. At the time of writing this, some months later, he is very poorly and our lives have changed utterly. My dynamic, energetic, inventive, warm, witty, wise, funny and practical husband has become wobbly, incoherent, lost and living in another world. He can no longer grasp the principles of Buddhism – or anything else, for that matter – and day by day I feel that I am losing him. He is slipping away from me and I have less and less companionship and connection with him, although I do frequently encourage him to take a mindfulness breath, and to be 'in the now', which soothes and helps him. And when we go to bed at night, I often guide him in following his breath to breathe in *metta* and light.

I feel my heart overflowing with love for him, as well as, at times, many other, mixed emotions: irritation, anger, fear, exhaustion, frustration, grief and loneliness. I have realized that the times when I feel most heart-broken are when I think of the past – all the amazing times we had together and the things we shared that will never happen again; or when I think of the future, without him as he was or without him at all.

When I realize that I am thinking of the past or the future, I get back into the present moment and notice the emotion, feel the pain of the thoughts and memories and often allow myself to cry, and then the pain really does ease and there is healing

Another thing I find helpful when I am feeling really sad is to turn yearning for – or mourning for – the past into a sense of gratitude for what was. I think to myself how grateful I am for what we experienced, for the time we had together, for the things we did. I feel blessed when I think about the projects we worked on together, our fantastic holidays, the birth of our wonderful children, the support he always gave me. He was someone who was always on my side, who loved me whatever. And I'm so grateful, too, for the way he introduced me to Buddhism and the retreats we held here. That is a lot to be grateful for, and I find that gratitude – like *metta* – is healing.

The more I keep bringing myself back into the present moment, accepting things as they are and just feeling the peace and strength of this moment, the more things simply seem to unfold for me. The help I need just suddenly comes to me without me apparently doing anything; it seems to arrive almost effortlessly. Life, as the monk told us, just seems to flow and for that I am deeply grateful.

This has happened to me so often that now, when I have a problem or a need or a question, I just go in meditation to that place of clarity and peace within and I know that I will be looked after, that all will be well and whatever I need will come to me.

I am so grateful to have discovered a reservoir of peace, strength, love and – yes, even joy – within myself. If you had told me this before, I would not have believed you. But the strength and the peace are almost tangible. They help me to be patient, accepting, loving, gentle and happy. With the mindfulness breath and meditation, I find I can keep getting to this place, which feels as if it is at the centre of my being.

The other day I came across a quote that describes it perfectly. It is by the monk's first Theravada teacher, Ajahn Chah, in his book *Still Forest Pool*:

'Try to be mindful, and let things take their natural course. Then your mind will become still in any surroundings, like a clear forest pool. All kinds of wonderful, rare animals will come to drink at the pool, and you will clearly see the nature of all things. You will see many strange and wonderful things come and go, but you will be still. This is the happiness of the Buddha.'

I hope you will find the teaching as helpful as I have done, whatever your own situation.

With much *metta*,

Rose Elliot

Rose Elliot MBE has authored over 60 vegetarian cookbooks that have made her a much-loved household name. Born in a spiritual centre run by her family, Rose started her career cooking for the visitors to the retreats there, and wrote her first book, *Simply Delicious*, in response to the many requests she had for her recipes. Although Rose moved away from the centre after some years, as she has described in this book, the spiritual environment in which she grew up, not only provided the springboard for her career, but made a lasting impression on her and sparked her own interest in spiritual matters that has now found expression in *I Met a Monk*. Nowadays, Rose's recipes spring from the happiness of her family life, cooking for her husband Robert, their three daughters, growing number of grandchildren, all vegetarian, and their wider circle of friends.

Rose has received many accolades and awards for her work including being shortlisted for the Glenfiddick Awards, and winning, best vegetarian cuisine book in the world by the

Gourmand World Cookbook Awards 2010. She has an honorary degree from the University of Winchester and was awarded the MBE, 'for services to vegetarian cookery' in 1999.

Rose is also as an accomplished astrologer, author of *Life Cycles*, and Fellow of the Association of Professional Astrologers International (FAPAI).

For more information, visit **www.roseelliot.com**

WATKINS

Sharing Wisdom Since
1893

The story of Watkins Publishing dates back to March 1893, when John M. Watkins, a scholar of esotericism, overheard his friend and teacher Madame Blavatsky lamenting the fact that there was nowhere in London to buy books on mysticism, occultism or metaphysics. At that moment Watkins was born, soon to become the home of many of the leading lights of spiritual literature, including Carl Jung, Rudolf Steiner, Alice Bailey and Chögyam Trungpa.

Today our passion for vigorous questioning is still resolute. With over 350 titles on our list, Watkins Publishing reflects the development of spiritual thinking and new science over the past 120 years. We remain at the cutting edge, committed to publishing books that change lives.

DISCOVER MORE ...

| Read our blog | Watch and listen to our authors in action | Sign up to our mailing list |

JOIN IN THE CONVERSATION

 WatkinsPublishing  @watkinswisdom

 WatkinsPublishingLtd  +watkinspublishing1893

Our books celebrate conscious, passionate, wise and happy living.
Be part of the community by visiting

www.watkinspublishing.com